In the Shadow of the Pulpit

To Sarah,
Respecting and
appreciating your
interest

In the Shadow of the Pulpit

An anecdotal autobiography

Ann and Joel Klein

Writers Club Press

San Jose New York Lincoln Shanghai

In the Shadow of the Pulpit
An anecdotal autobiography

Writers Club Press
an imprint of iUniverse, Inc.

For information address:
iUniverse, Inc.
5220 S. 16th St., Suite 200
Lincoln, NE 68512
www.iuniverse.com

This autobiography refers to actual locations, institutions, political systems, and persons. Although inspired by actual events the places, characters, and persons are unnamed to protect their identities and preserve the rights of living or deceased people to confidentiality.

ISBN: 0-595-20696-4

Printed in the United States of America

We dedicate this story of our lives
to the source of our lives,
the memory of our dear parents
who started us on the path which we then chose to follow

CONTENTS

A Comment

Joel Klein followed up his full length book with an anecdotal autobiography co-authored with his talented and charming wife, Ann, revealing the story of their remarkable life. It is the tale of a man and wife who experienced and survived many of the horrors of the twentieth century, including concentration camps and death sentences, and emerged from the ordeal stronger and more committed to a life of morals and religious service to others. *The Shadow of the Pulpit* is a remarkable memoir of two remarkable people on life's journey toward goodness, growing and changing as they go, but always lovingly. This is a fine book, and candidate for a number of book awards.

—Richard A. Gabriel, Ph.D.
—Author of: *The Warrior Pharaoh*
and
Sebastian's Cross

OTHER WORKS BY JOEL T. KLEIN

Through the Name of God, A New Road to the Origin of Judaism and Christianity, 2001

Bialik Hebrew Day School. Metropolitan Toronto, Ont. Canada. A Monograph. *Dor LeDor, Studies in the History of Jewish Education in Israel and the Diaspora. Vol. XVII.* 2000

Mein Ende des Zweiten Weltkrieges, *Besiegt, befreit…Zeitzungen erinnern sich an das Kriegsende 1945,* 1995

A Story Along the Journey, *Stories Along the Journey,Spiritual and Theological Reflections for Pastoral Counselors,* 1993

A Jew Looks at the Two-Thousand Year Encounter, *Sharing Shalom, A Process for Local Interfaith Dialogue between Christians and Jews,* 1989

Habakuk 3:13–A Problematic Verse, *Dor le-Dor,* 1985

INTRODUCTION

Welcome to the reading of our story that presents parts of our lives, vignettes and anecdotes.

In the chapters ahead you will read about us and others who are not named or identified. We omitted names and identification deliberately although it was not even necessary because some seem to be like yourself while others are very different. In the end you may realize that despite all the differences, we all are alike. Beyond identities and differences there is in all a common core of self, our essential humanity. When we identify with that inner core, respecting and honoring it in others as well as in ourselves, we arrive at a true appreciation of the ultimate goodness in all of us.

You may find joy and happiness, fulfilment and disappointment, struggle, and achievement of peace in our stories. In one form or another, these elements make up the life story of everyone.

We consider this book our gift to you. We hope that the recognition of our common basic humanness will be a block in building peace in the private and communal lives of all of us.

RETROSPECTION

I was born in 1923 and named Tibor Klein in Hungary. My career as a rabbi began before I was born. My mother came from a long line of rabbinic families. In my consciousness, I was aware that before my birth my parents decided to continue that family tradition. They agreed that if their first born would be a male child, they would direct and train him to grow up into the rabbinic calling. I recall that from my earliest years I have been groomed to become a rabbi.

Living in a small town where there was no chance for a formal Jewish education, my parents made sure that I would learn. From age three, to pursue my Hebrew studies I walked five days a week to the home of the local shochet-dayyan, the man who provided the ritual slaughtering and made decisions in doubtful cases of religious observance.

I did not know much about who and what a rabbi was. But I saw the priest of the small town where those early years of my life were spent. I liked his long black robe. If someone asked me what I wanted to become when I will have grown up, my answer was, "a catholic priest."

A bitter experience partially changed my childish plan about becoming a priest. In the country where Roman Catholicism was the state religion, the first day of school was observed in the Catholic church. At age six my parents did not allow me to attend the opening day exercises of my first grade studies there. I hid under the counter of the only grocery store where I frequently spent my free time helping the owner. For my help I received copies of the different advertisement papers that came in small pads. The owner used them to add up the price of the purchased items and gave them to the customers as receipts. I received them to build my collection. I recall that around noon time I hid behind the door of the store and peeked at the street. I saw the back of the priest as he walked away from the church.

The next day, as on all school days, the first hour was spent on religious education. The priest entered the classroom and for an icebreaker asked the students to introduce themselves and state their religion after their name.

Including me there were only two Jewish students in the class. We were seated in the double desk at the back of the room. Hearing that all the other students were catholic, we were afraid to be different and announced ourselves to be catholic. As the first subject of study we learned to make the cross on our chests. In the afternoon my mother was interested to know what I learned on the first day of school. I told her about making the cross. She became anxious and told me that the next day she would take me to school. She did. She talked to the priest and told him that I was Jewish. The other boy frightened, stood up and declared that he was Jewish, too. My mother was clear about her decision and stated that I cannot participate in catholic religious education. She left and the priest became angry. He sternly demanded that the two of us get up and go to the front of the room. In his exhortation he scolded us, and since we sinned, he meted out the punishment that every day, while he was teaching the class, the two of us would kneel on corn spread at the edge of the podium on which his desk and chair were set up. It took about a half-a-year for our parents to find a way to have us excused from the class, but there was no instructor to teach Jewish studies. Since I was born after the cut off date of registering for first grade, at that time I was more than seven years old. I learned the Hebrew alphabet at age three and read Hebrew fluently. I was appointed to be the teacher of the few Jewish children in the school until a suitable person was brought to town.

My parents were concerned about the education of their two sons. When I finished first grade, they moved us to a suburb of the capital city and enrolled me in the public school. As a Jewish boy, I had no difficulty in second grade. In the third grade I had a new teacher. My mother came to school and asked my teacher to allow me to meet our religious requirement to cover my head while offering my silent prayer and having my lunch. The teacher told her, "If this is what you want, send your son to a parochial school."

Although the tuition fee was high in the parochial school, my parents made sacrifices, and my formal religious education began.

The rabbi of our congregation had a great influence on me from my early age. He was tall, very handsome. I looked at him on the pulpit, and his voice sounded to me like Moses speaking on Mount Sinai. He influenced several of us to get interested in the rabbinate. Under his guidance from our city fourteen young men were studying for the rabbinate when I completed the ninth grade in high school. I began spending more of my free time in his office that in my home. He introduced us to the practical aspects of the rabbinate. He gave us opportunities to learn. He taught us when we were able to listen to him and catch glimpses of his wisdom. He taught us when he patiently studied religious texts with us. Before I reached age thirteen he guided me already. At my Bar Mitzvah celebration in his dedication talk he outlined a way of life for me in the presence of the congregation.

To be accepted to the rabbinical school there was a rigorous test to pass. The year I applied, twelve of the 120 applicants were accepted. Although delving into the rule of its grammar was my favorite pastime, I got an unsatisfactory mark on my Latin exam. At my second trial a year later I was accepted into the high school department of the Jewish Theological Seminary of Hungary.

Our rabbi started me and the other Seminary students to be in the public eye from an early age. At the study session following the Saturday afternoon services we, seminary students, took turns to deliver short discourses, words of Torah.

World War II and the European Holocaust interrupted my education. My bright and shining dream of being a leader to work with people to enlighten them as a rabbi turned into a dark experience.

The usual privilege of being exempt from military service as a theological student was not extended to me. The first experience denied me the sense of dignity and respect that are due to a human being which I made a lifetime goal to give everybody. When I reported for service and moved to the first line at the registration table, the officer asked, "What's the name of the whore who gave birth to you?"

This kind of treatment continued through that shadowy dark period of my life. When I was asked about my training and occupation and I answered that I was a rabbinic student, I received a heavy slap across my face with the accompanying harshly yelled statement, "There are rabbis no more, only dogs, and dogs don't deserve to be in the same place as humans!"

But on one occasion I was acknowledged as "rabbi." I was chosen to move the dead bodies out of the camp to the outskirts of the town and bury them around midnight in the forest with the strict instruction not to leave any sign that there was a grave there. In the morning I was called to answer my crime. In the dark of the winter night, we did not see that the burial hole was not filled to level with the ground. As the punishment for this crime my hands and feet were tied to a cudgel and I had to sit twelve hours in that position near the barracks where one of the officers sat comfortably close to the stove that kept him warm.

I kept my dream alive. After the war, I returned to Hungary from the concentration camps and resumed my simultaneous studies at the Seminary and at the University of Science in Budapest where I earned my Ph.D. in Semitic Languages, Ancient Oriental History and Psychology.

I recall those long years of studies and my teachers with fondness, yet I find it difficult to choose the master who had the greatest influence on my life. Certainly our local rabbi, a martyr of the atrocities that he suffered by the hands of the Holocaust perpetrators, led me to the gateways of true learning. I recall three of the numerous teachers and professors as my masters who shared the depth of their knowledge with their students. Some of them were trained in German scholarly institutions. All were influenced by the analytical thinking of their professors. The three, who stand out in my memories, were different. They taught us to think systematically. They emphasized the importance of textual research. Their focus was a methodology to pay close attention to the details, but they spread our horizon wider and showed us how to integrate the pieces into the global picture. They taught by instruction and their example that gathering data was not enough. Above all they required us to learn to think.

While a student in the last year of my formal studies I was a teacher of Religion, Jewish History, Bible and Hebrew at one of the Jewish high schools in Budapest. One year prior to ordination, I was elected chief rabbi of the south- central section of Hungary. Three years later, I was elected chief rabbi of northwestern Hungary. I served these two districts until the uprising against the tyranny of Soviet occupation.

In the initial days of the revolution the fighting was purely for ideological changes. But after the early days inciting speeches and acts of antisemitic venom marred the purity of the revolution. In the hope that it would save the members of my congregation from the fashionable atrocities, and because also I wanted to see the end of the communist oppression, I supported the revolution financially. For these activities, I received a severe sentence from a Russian military court. With help from personal friends, I was freed from the prison and was able to rejoin my family who escaped from Hungary and immigrated to the United States.

Here I recall a dream of my youth. In the history of my native country I learned that one of the most outstanding political leaders of the country in 1840s came to the United States to raise funds to support the revolution against the Habsburg dynasty. He spoke eloquently to American audiences. While learning about his activities, I dreamed of learning a language besides my mother tongue to that perfection that I could deliver public speeches. I came to this country with the knowledge of one word and one English phrase (mispronounced). I reached the realisation of that dream. For a few months I worked in blue collar positions during the day, and studied English at night with special instructors in small groups. I was able to accomplish what I believed my family tradition expected of me. Six months after my arrival at these shores, I was elected Hebrew teacher and assistant rabbi of a New England congregation.

After thirty years on the pulpit, I rechannelled my energies and became a State licensed Pastoral Psychotherapist, a Marriage and Family Therapist, and a certified sex counselor. I have taught and lectured at colleges. I learned about problems and worked with individuals, couples, and families to search for solutions.

Many of these experiences would be worthwhile to mention as legacies of my life time. I mention only one. When I was young, inexperienced and overzealous, I allowed myself to be guided by the principle that 'If I don't have a job, I can't maintain a family.'

It was my great fortune that some threatening events of our lives taught me to rearrange the words without changing the principle, 'If I don't have a family, I can't maintain a job.'

WHERE I COME FROM

As a woman I had no training for the rabbinate not even for becoming and being a rabbi's wife.

I find it difficult to describe the early periods of my life. My life began in 1930 in Hungary. I have very few memories of the early years of my life. I was robbed of my childhood. I feel a gaping hole in its place. I know that my father was a traveling insurance salesman. To assure our livelihood he was away from home almost for the entire length of the week. He was devoted to his religious belief, but at times it became increasingly difficult to live by his beliefs. It was hard to find a job. Three consecutive anti-Jewish laws pushed an ever growing number of Jews out of their jobs and positions. My father lost his insurance salesman employment. The possibility of observing the Sabbath and our holidays seemed disappearing. My father made everything possible to maintain the religious atmosphere in our home. His siblings, who were much stricter than he, would not even think that their brother was breaking the law, and put him under great pressure. He could not find steady work, he did odd jobs, he tutored children for a very meager reimbursement.

The conditions created by the anti-Jewish laws did not produce much change in the ways our household was managed . While my father was still traveling my mother took over the role of both parents. She worked with us on our homework assignments. She taught us to work with our hands, just as she was working literally day and night to supplement the income my father could produce.

For mother our religious education was of high priority. She wanted us to attend the Jewish day school. She was strict in our religious upbringing and observance yet for the sake of a better education agreed to enroll us in the more liberal school that was attached to the non-orthodox synagogue.

While my father could produce a steady income, we had no serious monetary problems. The tuition fee, although with difficulty, was paid every month on time. When the circumstances turned rougher, I dreaded the first day of each month. I knew that the principal would enter the first class of the day and in his deep threatening voice look at me in the presence of all my classmates and say, "You there, scram and do not return until your parents paid your tuition." I developed a fear and resentment.

My face turned red, my head was hanging. I did not dare to look at the girls in the class. I lowered my head and my eyes fell upon the floor. Close to the wall with that lowered head, I walked out of the room. In the corridor I met my younger sister who, too, was exposed to the very same demeaning experience.

In our home the Saturday afternoons were very tense times. My father, tired and lacking the usual amount of nicotine, became increasingly demanding of my brothers. He was probably fearful and felt guilty that he could not give all he wanted to his children. So he expected perfection. My father reacted with angry responses to any mistake the boys made when he checked on their weekly studies.

Combined with my school experiences these Saturday exercises diminished my interest in studies in general. I became ever more withdrawn, shy, and showed not much enthusiasm toward being sociable with youngsters and adults. My pride turned into shame. I sometimes wondered who I was and why I had to live under those circumstances.

I still attended the school after my parents found the money somewhere to pay our tuition and continued to attend the Saturday afternoon Junior Congregation services. I recall that we had a young assistant rabbi who was in charge of these services. One of the brightest spots of the weeks was this service when we saw him on the pulpit and after services we girls could talk about him. Most of us had a crush on him.

The first three years of my high school education were clouded by these events, but occasionally some sunshine broke through. The summer vacations eased the almost constant pain I felt in school. It was the routine in my house that no matter how difficult our life was, my mother managed to have some of my cousins to live with us in the city to get their education. In the summer it was our turn to spend a few weeks with my father's somewhat better-to-do sisters away from the city in their rural environment. My aunts on my mother's side of the family loved and spoiled us, but it was not all that way with some of the other relatives. My father had four brothers. They showed little sensitivity to the nature and needs of us young girls. As I mentioned before they were more extreme in their religious practices than my father or mother. Some of their behavior spoiled not us but the good time we might have had. One of my uncles was critical of the way our parents allowed us to dress. Their daughters wore long skirts and long sleeve blouses. They demanded conformity. We were expected to have the same attire. On one occasion my uncle lost his temper since I wore a plain sun dress without sleeves. I showed too much bare skin. It was too much for his standards.

This was the one incident when I saw my father stand up to his brothers and sternly stated that it was up to him what his children would wear during the winter or the summer.

I am writing about these incidents as an adult. I cannot place myself in that situation now and feel like when I was a child. But I can recall that I was wondering whether a God could care about my dress, about the length of its sleeves, and whether religion was all about this. I imagined that God had other things to do. Through the eyes of the child I saw Him sitting on his golden chair and watching over the well being and suffering of the people. I could not believe that the pieces of a girl's clothing were really important to Him. Clothing was a source of joy for me when before Passover and Rosh Hashanah my parents made every effort to dress us in new outfits that added to the centrality of observance and the holiday spirit. But I am convinced that the experience in my uncle's house certainly left a mark on me, on my thinking, my beliefs and attitude toward observances.

Not connected with clothing, I had my encounter with my personal God. I realized what a gift He gave me in my mother.

We were the very few whose deported transport was turned away from Auschwitz since at the time we arrived the barracks were filled beyond their capacities. We were dispatched to a small Austrian town where the farmers requested labor force. We were sent to an elderly man's household as an intact family. This lucky strike of ours continued when we were transported to a camp remaining together the same family unit. I was not fourteen yet. Due to lack of food, lack of clothing, lack of hygiene I became very sick. I was not thinking of the goodness of God. I was sick I wished I could die.

When my mother saw my depression, she very gently led me, her sick and weak child, out of the barrack. It was a sunny day. First she was silent, then she turned toward me, looked into my eyes, and began talking softly with a determination in her voice. She asked me to look up to the blue sky and see the radiant sun. When I followed her suggestion, she asked me to turn the other way. Again I raised my eyes and saw the chimney of the crematorium, smoke bellowing out of it darkening and blocking the blue patch of the sky. For a while, that seemed like eternity, we were silent, then she said, "You are sick, you still have a choice. You can decide to live, or you can decide to die and go up in smoke like many others who turned into ashes in the crematorium."

I am alive. My mother gave me life twice. Once in the small town in Hungary, and the second time in a concentration camp.

The End of a Beginning

1943

It was the twenty-first year of my life. In the fall of the previous year, I had made a decision already about my future. I was a freshman at the University of Science in Budapest, Hungary. The law of numerus clausus, the restriction that decided the number of Jewish students accepted to the universities, restricted the courses these students were allowed to choose. I decided on psychology, ancient oriental history, and Semitic languages.

The atmosphere, that surrounded us in the city where we lived and at school, was filled with uncertainties. Due to Jew-bashing and physical atrocities I missed several days of school. But I continued. I did not give up. I hoped for brighter days to come.

In my hometown the tension was rising. People, who could not prove their citizenship to the satisfaction of the government agencies, were removed overnight from their homes along with their family members, no one knew how, whereto, and for what purpose. The rumor mills cranked out information, constantly quoting well-informed, highly-placed, reliable sources.

One explanation seemed acceptable: those who were removed might not have been natives of our land. Their families might have immigrated from other countries. Our families usually could prove that way back several generations they were citizens. Our ancestors had fought for that land. We, too, were ready to defend it. Many of my generation already had made the supreme sacrifice in defense of our nation. Surely, the government would not abandon us. We were certain that we would be protected. We were fed by our eternal optimism. We were sure about ourselves. We

11

were convinced that our home was in our homeland. We were at home. We never broke the law. We believed that it could happen to the "foreigners". They were different. Anyway, in our belief, we were safe. We could not be treated like that. That could not happen to us.

Then came that unforgettable Sunday in 1944. A tremendous calm hung over us. Something that could be there only before a devastating storm. The radio silenced for a while, then martial music came on the airwaves.

Shortly after noon, tanks roared with their monotonous, but threatening engine noise rambling on the main city arteries with such a force that the cobble stones that provided a solid surface for the regular traffic, moved out of their places, turning the streets into rocky roads, as if foretelling the paths of the future that lay ahead of us.

Although some classes were cancelled, a few of us still lingered in the Seminary building. Everything was quiet. No one spoke a loud word. Two German officers in their immaculate uniforms entered the gate. Their short inspection resulted in a two-word declaration, "Zu alt." We had no idea what the two words "too old" meant. Later on, we learned that the men were Eichman and Wesenmayer. They were looking for a suitable building that would hold selected hostages before deportation.

It did not matter that originally they judged the building too old for their purpose. It became a holding Lager.

At night on the way home, German soldiers and local police stepped into the street cars, checked the passengers' papers and at times uttered harsh sounds, "Jude, Absteigen!" They left the train. They moved their hostages, nobody knew where.

The days passed filled with mixed feelings, fear and optimism. The former defeated the latter on the day when even those who had only one grandparent born of a Jewish father or mother, were ordered to wear a permanently attached two-and-a-half inch yellow star on their outer piece of garment.

I lived across the street from the public bath house. German soldiers spent their free time there, or stopped there while on patrol duty. I passed them on my side of the street trembling and walking like one who wanted to disappear in the walls of the houses to escape their watching eyes.

Ten days later, my call-up paper arrived, ordering me to leave immediately on the next available train to report at the recruiting center located in a far distant town that not long before was part of another country. I confidently left my home. I trusted my government that issued me certificates that granted me the privilege to be exempt from military service as a theological student. I did not say "good-bye" only "so-long" to my family. The trip was planned as a three-day excursion. That was the last time I saw my mother.

My exempt status was not honored; instead when I reported at the registration table, I was asked what the name of the whore was who gave me birth.

Humiliation, degradation, the destruction of the minutest remaining self-esteem became my lot along with many other millions. There is no need to enumerate the torture, the hunger, the inhuman condition while on death marches, the senseless forced labor, the illnesses, the slaps across the face that were supposed to serve as medication, the weight loss, the pain, no family, no friends, no news. There is no need to describe the enduring hope to live for the day of liberation and the constant fear that frequently suggested that it might have been better to be dead than to suffer under conditions which could not be called life.

When the desire rather to die overcame my miserable existence, my mother's words, written on her last postcard, instilled in me an immeasurable will to continue the struggle. On the day before she was carried to her untimely death by being murdered in a gas chamber, she wrote those words that echoed in my ears, "My dear son, we don't know what the future will bring, yet perform your duties faithfully under any circumstances."

I had no idea what my duties were. I lost my feelings of allegiance. I had only one duty. It was to survive and be reunited with my family. I did not know yet that it would never happen.

Despite all this, one day offered a last chance to realize our hopes. It seemed the end was nearing. In a foreign land, still surrounded by the hated uniforms, flame throwers, cannons, guns, and all kinds of artillery fire, a ray of hope was shining with the promise that survival was possible. Our unit, several times decimated, was in disarray. It was decision making time again: either move toward the country with the possibility to work undetected on a farm until the end, or walk into the metropolis, attempting to evade the last minute blood hunt for those whose planned extermination was not yet executed. To our surprise an old man stopped and in our mother tongue inquired about the identity of the three men who, filled with trembling and uncertainty, sought refuge on the steps of the Stadttheater. We risked a lie. We gave a false identity. The old man was probably frightened and hoped to gain some good points that later would save his skin. He offered asylum for us, the three men of different ages. The hide-out, an intact room, not visible behind the two-story high debris of a bombed-out house, became our home. It was the castle of a physician before an air raid made him homeless. In that dusty room, we experienced the first sign of humanity amongst the acts of bestiality to which we had been exposed for quite a while already. We did not raise questions about the motive behind those acts. We had a roof over our head, our rescuer even shared some of their meager food supply with us, the fugitives. We had something to eat, we even slept. Still it was a ten-day period filled with terror, but above all again with that hope that survival was possible. It was in quite a contrast with the first night of our escape. By fear-inducing coincidence, we spent that night in the home of a Lutwaffe pilot whose wife, the Hausmeisterin allowed us to stay on the floor of their kitchen. Then we could not accept as reality that after their dinner, he played a recorded song, "Es geht alles forüber." I felt that there was a maybe. Maybe, all that would pass.

We lived the day of that miracle. In the morning, the old man climbed over the rubble, and in a whisper he said; "It's over; the Russians reached our neighborhood."

Two more days were spent without seeing the sun. I lived those two days with the thought which I did not dare to put into words for ten years.

Maybe after the years of legalized deprivation, total dehumanization, we could become humans again.

A daring move took me out of our hiding place, and what a change I saw. Throughout our wondering in the city before the old man led us away, the streets were swarming with uniformed men and with women proudly displaying their arm bands. And now…every door and every gate bore words chalked on them, "Nur Zivilen." My amazement, combined with anger, increased my fear. I could not believe that attitudes changed overnight. I saw what was on the surface, but I feared what was hidden under that facade. I could not accept that an instant metamorphosis took place. I still would not dare to reveal my identity

At the same time, I imagined what I truly wanted to see. It was like a dream turned into reality. My eyes, turned inwardly, saw a world with "no soldiers" anymore, "only civilians." My imagination pictured peaceful citizens who were ready to build a new world instead of a new world order.

Although clouds covered the April sky and the sun did not shine, the inner sunshine warmed my heart, and the thought of a brighter future my mind. Yet, I could hardly walk. I felt like a drunk although I did not take any intoxicating substance. My difficulty to walk was not the result of the accident in which my legs were burnt by Diesel fuel about five weeks before. I weighed a mere sixty-six pounds. Every step required a great effort. Walking was difficult, yet I felt like I was flying. I was free. I wanted to see the place from where my homeland was ruled for centuries. My direction was the Burg in Vienna. My heart was pounding. The "Heftling," the prisoner, the condemned was walking through the city streets like a tourist, planning some site seeing. Finally, there was in front of my eyes the great iron gate, beyond it the beautifully manicured garden. Suddenly, my pounding heart pumped all my blood into my head. A fainting spell overtook my entire being, like having been struck by a hammer on my head. A sign was there, yellow with black lettering, "Hunde und Juden verboten." Anger? No. Rage. My hand formed a tightly clinched fist ready to strike. There was time to chalk the words, "Nur

Zivilen" on the doors and on the gates to protect the fearful, but no time to remove the sign of shame. Liberation was there, but no freedom for me. I knew that there would have been no punishment for entering the garden, but I could not carry myself beyond the threshold which that gate marked. I lived the day to be liberated, but was not free from the debasement of eleven years. The memories broke all the flood gates.

"Hunde und Juden." In the stone quarry, that twelve-year old, the master of our lives and deaths, stood guard with his machine gun and his giant pampered dog, instilling an ever-present terror in us. Dogs and Jews were on different levels of dignity. Then, I wished to be equated with that dog's care, but in front of the Burg's gate, the humiliation struck my heart deep again.

This was my first and unfortunate impression of liberation.

Then while quietly walking back to the room of hiding, my mind turned to the home which I left, to the members of my family whose fate became hidden, so unknown. Filled with hope, I was longing.

For me, the war was over. Was it for them, too? lingered the unanswerable question. The only desire that fueled my will to continue living was the wish to leave the city, the imagined site of my tourist visit, just the wish to go home. The new experience reinforced my fear. I still feared to admit that I was Jewish.

Five days later, on foot, I began my homeward journey. A few blocks from our hiding place, in the middle of the city, a large crowd appeared in our eyesight. Uniformed men hovered all around them. But nothing to fear. These uniforms were not those of our oppressors. The uniforms suggested they were our liberators. Yet another foreign language for us. A soldier yelled, grabbed my arm, and tossed me in a group of people lined up in military fashion. I was protesting loudly in words and silently in my thoughts. I convinced myself that they were our liberators, and subsequently they would know what fate was meted out for us. I picked up a few words from their compatriots when they came to our hometown hoping to escape their fate. I hoped that the knowledge of the Russian word for JEW would save me. That soldier knew a Jew only from speaking Yiddish. I did not speak that language. For him, I was not a Jew. The march of about two thousand POW-s began, I amongst them. The first week of freedom ended for me.

Again, these were big times to plan quickly and make fateful decisions. Behind me was the German plan for the final solution, ahead of me the prospect of a POW camp, almost certain death. I wanted to live. Accompanied by the two other men with whom I went into hiding, I tricked the guards. We escaped.

New horizons opened up for me.

What to do? On what foundation shall I rebuild my life that was lying in ruins? First, I had to decide where I belonged. I never considered myself politically inclined. I certainly was not, I could not be a Nazi, but I was not a Communist either. But my survival suggested a demand to declare myself. I was considering the ideology of the social-democrats of my country before the war. I considered it a comfortable resolution. That affiliation seemed to offer a chance to work for the realization of another idea I had when I wrote an essay in the ninth grade. I had described a world in which free trade allowed the nations to share their wealth and exchange what they had for what they needed. My fascist teacher sought my expulsion from school since he detected communist ideas in my thinking.

In contrast, what a joy it was when the League of Nations ceased to exist and the United Nations carried even in its name the hope of my idealism and dreams. The dance on the streets, the euphoria of the world fell in line with my imagination. The war ended for the entire world, not only for me.

My idealism proved to be short lived. I returned to my country at the end of war, and a few years later on the bayonets of the Red Army the communist minority came into power and crushed the social-democrats.

Probably some similar or identical hopes of the German youth were also crushed the same way my dreams evaporated. Instead of a world united, fully and totally cooperating with each other, their country was divided and in the two sections two political systems were pitched against the other.

In reality, for all practical purposes, the hostilities of the war ended for the world, but as I realized, it did not for me. My hopes slowly died. As the enormity of my loss, most of my family members perished, the atrocities committed by humans' inhumanity became known. My war just had begun. I made a vow never to set foot on German soil. I still adhere to it strictly. I traveled through Germany three times, but my foot did not touch German soil. One experience seemed to strengthen that vow. One midnight in 1957, my train stopped at the Frankfurt am Main railroad station. I lowered the window to catch some fresh air. I had the unexpected chance to listen to a conversation between a uniformed railroad worker on the platform and a civilian who traveled on the same train. The man in the uniform expressed his disappointment in Hitler that he did not finish the final solution to the Jewish question. This conversation brought back memories. Shortly after my return from deportation in 1945, I visited the house which I left to report for service in 1944. The superintendent of the house looked at me with a surprise in his eyes and said, "I am truly sorry, more of you came back than left." Here they were again, my shattered dreams and the destructive reality.

My war did not end. I was angry at both men, the uniformed railroad worker and the superintendent, my anger became generalized, at the whole world. I was angry with those who stood by silently when the genocide was pursued with supreme intensity and with those who were later dissatisfied with the outcome. I was angry with the Germans and with those who so willingly cooperated with them. Reliving the war was much harder than to live through it. I was and I am still driven to read everything I can lay my hand on about the Holocaust. I defy my pain and I watch every documentary that deals with the Holocaust. I do not understand my obsession that drove me back to one of the labor camps to exhume and identify the bodies I was forced to bury.

Attempting to understand my pain and use it for some purpose, as a psychotherapist I decided to work with Vietnam veterans. I believed that I could empathize with their suffering. The realization of my idea was only partial. They were talking about horrifying flashbacks. I could not identify my experience with their recurring rage. I had no idea what a flashback was until my life changed. Our first grandchild was born. I loved him. I planned to give him all the gentleness that was in me. One day, I picked up the baby. The geyser of my rage erupted. That was it, the flashback. My whole body trembled. I feared the loss of my physical strength. I feared I would drop the child. The memories gushed from their tightly sealed wells. I had never experienced anything like that, not when I held our own children. I saw babies thrown up in the air and caught on the point of the SS bayonets. I saw them cut into pieces in the horrified presence of parents and bystanders. I saw the babies in their mothers' arms carried to their death. I lived my war, and I relive my war again and again. I live it in my dreams and my nightmares. I live it when I dream that the Gestapo comes for me, and wanting to escape, I am trapped. I live my war, when in my dream I seek help, I search for someone who would hide me, and there is none to extend a helping hand.

The war ended, and I learned a few things. I understand the German people. I do not hold grudges against those young people who did not know it differently. They were taught, indoctrinated. They believed in races, in pure blood, in inferiority, and superiority. This was the only doctrine they knew.

They were trained, desensitized in order to silence their conscience in the face of brutality. I don't even believe there is to forgive anything. But I hold on to my anger when I see what the new generation is doing. I hold on to my anger seeing that the new generation was denied the right to know what atrocities their ancestors committed, seeing that their textbooks delegated more than a decade of history to the size of a footnote, seeing that it has been possible to allow chauvinism and nationalism to raise their ugly heads again.

The war ended, and I learned many things. Now upon awakening every morning, I consider myself blessed. I have been granted another day. I am living on borrowed time. Life showers me with gifts that could have been denied from me. I talked with many survivors. They told me about their broken faith and their lost belief. They shared with me their struggle to find justice in the world and a belief in a God. They ask where their God was then, and if there was a God how could He (or She) stand by with closed eyes and allow all that to happen.

The war affected me differently. I had not raised the question how those millions were allowed to die. After the war, my issue became this: I was not better, and not worse than those millions who perished. They are not here. What is the mission for which I was saved? I will search for the answer as long as I live. Yet, something became crystal clear to me. When I am asked how I could live a normal life, raise a family, work in a professional capacity after all I had been through, I give only one answer: without those past experiences, I would not be the same person who I am now.

Unknown Details

Ann, 1949

As I am sitting on the bus to visit my relatives, I am wondering what my mother had in mind to send me away to visit family members for the Passover holiday. She loved to have the nuclear family around her table at that time of the year.

I was preoccupied with these thoughts and my expectations throughout the long bus ride. But when the bus stopped at my destination, it was time to wake up from my daydreaming.

One of the relatives waited for me and led me to their home.

It was close to lunch time. The day before Passover was the busiest time with the holiday preparations. Lunch usually was the simplest possible. To my surprise the table was set quite elaborately. I wondered what it was all about.

The answer was not immediate. There were people around the table. A series of introductions followed since some of them did not know me, and, in turn, I did not know them.

Finally, I could relax, I thought, and I could sit down. I had enough of the introductions and meeting new people. It was not my favorite activity anyway.

But it was not meant that way. Just when I thought we can start a conversation and fill the gaps that occurred since our last contact, more company arrived. A young man entered the room accompanied by a young woman, approximately my age, if not somewhat older.

I looked at the people and judging their comfort, it seemed that they were familiar with both of them. I became somewhat overwhelmed and even experienced some discomfort. The people were not surprised by the two new guests' coming. The young man was there with someone whom he knew before. I was the guest, almost ignored.

The introduction did not mean much to me. It only added two more names to the list.

Gratefully the traditional lunch was served. As the custom dictated, no conversation during the courses of the meal. But as shy girls usually do, I lifted my eyes a few times and watched that man from the corner of my eyes with some curiosity. He behaved more controlled than the others around the table. A few times, I discovered that he looked at me, too. He was not flirting, but there was something in his winks that made me curious.

I was glad that there were breaks between the simple courses of the meal. I could listen to the conversation and attempt to figure out relationships.

The conversation was not the chit-chatty information exchange between acquaintances mixed with some gossip about the people of the town. Some of the ways it went, reminded me of Saturday noontime meals in my home when my father was still alive. He and my brothers concentrated on the study matters the boys dealt with during the past week. The conversation here, too, was about Jewish law, customs, chapters of the weekly Torah reading, and significantly, rather then making declarative statements, frequently questions were raised. At this place, too, like in my home where the elder, my father questioned the boys. Almost everybody, older than the young man, raised questiones directed to him. He did not seem very concerned. His answers flew seamlessly.

But where was I? I was an eighteen-year-old woman who came to visit relatives. I had to listen to the discussion of subjects that were far from the center of my interests, I heard exchanges of opinions which were similar to those which I heard at adult education classes.

This is not why I came here for at least eight more days. If this would go on, I will be bored, out of my skull.

I hoped I was not misreading something. When this young man spoke, he seemed confident although his words were accompanied by a sheepish smile. With the smile, I caught his dimples. They looked very appealing to me. His dignified, respect-demanding, stern demeanor softened. My dislike of his behavior softened.

The lunch came to an end. It was my time to ask questions. My cousin acted nonchalant. She told me that the stranger was the new rabbi of the congregation. After his election, he had moved in about nine months before. He took the pulpit of the once-prestigious, but now decimated congregation. He became the first rabbi to lead the congregation after the Holocaust. She told me that he came to that congregation after a very difficult time. His best friend for many years applied before him, was invited for two interviews, and was turned down.

She also mentioned that although the congregation was satisfied with his job performance, he had some inner struggles, that he became a competitor to his four-year older friend whom he admired and followed ever since they got acquainted.

"But what do you have to do with him?", I asked my cousin. She pointed at the house across the walkway. She provided some history. The building, that the congregation owned as the rabbi's home, was occupied by a family which moved in after the Jews of the city were closed into the ghetto and deported to Auschwitz. It was the case in all the Jewish homes. Some people who returned from the concentration camps needed to find temporary housing. The building she showed me, was part of the congregation's offices at that time occupied by a man, his wife and a son who could not return to their home. The Temple's board of directors decided to place the single rabbi in one of the rooms in that house.

He was single, not a man in the kitchen, he was not even given a kitchen. Since he strictly adhered to the dietary laws, he arranged to have his meals in my cousin's home whose husband served as the cantor of the congregation.

I listened to the story, but was not really interested. I was there on vacation, leaving behind me the patients, the hospital, the ward, the nurses, the nursing supervisor, and even the noise of the big city where I was in training for my future profession.

My bus ride was quite long. I wished to have an after lunch siesta and enjoy the quiet. But even that was not meant to be.

The young rabbi escorted his companion to the bus station, returned, but not to his room. He just stopped by. For what? Soon it became known. He asked me to take a stroll with him that he could point out the landmarks of the small southern-Hungarian city near the Yugoslavian border.

Not free from the concern about theological excursions, I reluctantly, but quite willingly agreed. The stroll and the conversation turned out to be pleasant. When we stopped at a bronze statue, I showed not much enthusiasm toward the story of the famous traveler who hailed from the city and went half way around the globe to find sister languages of Hungarian. The beautifully built and maintained catholic church did not catch my imagination either. The river side with the stroking breezes was more intriguing. I returned to the home of my relatives. He went to his residence.

At night I sat at the Seder table with questions and frequently changing emotions. I was glad that he did not come to share the holiday eve with us. He went to conduct the community Seder. But at times my thoughts left the room and I sought some answers to my questions. I rather entertained those than the questions and answers recorded in the Hagadah, the book that tells the story of the Israelites' liberation from Egypt.

In the morning, the rabbi and the cantor headed to the beautiful temple on the adjacent lot. It was not customary for women to attend services, so I remained in the house.

On the second night of Passover he asked me again if I was willing to take a walk. I played the hard to get, and offered a definite no. My excuse sounded very legitimate. I reminded him that the Seder meal ended late.

In reality I was thinking that I went there to have a restful vacation and not to keep the rabbi's company strolling around town.

I went with him on the third night. We sat down on one of the benches on the riverside. He talked. I mostly listened. He appeared to be romantic. He looked at the stars, then into my eyes. He named some of the constellations, told me how much he loved the beautiful sunny days, the azure blue sky, and gazing at the nighttime skies with the stars.

On the way back to my cousin's we took a small detour. He took me to the street where the rabbi's house stood and said that when he got married the congregation would move the persons who resided there and that house would be his home.

While he was talking enthusiastically about the details, I realized that he reached for my hand and gently but firmly did not let it go.

I was not sure of him. He asked me to take walks with him. I asked myself where the girl was who came with him for lunch. He never mentioned what his relationship was with her. I did not want to become the fifth wheel in his vehicle. But I was too shy to ask. It remained like an unspoken secret.

I went back to my relatives. Nothing unusual. We retired for the night. For me the question raised by the youngest at the Seder table remained unanswered, "Was that night different from all the other nights?"

In the morning, my cousin and her husband, the cantor, looked at me with an uninterested facial expression raising just one question, "Did you enjoy your walk?"

With similar neutrality I replied, "Yes it was nice, but it was a rabbinic walk, I listened and he talked a lot."

I was really hoping that they would talk about him. They knew him for nine months already. They knew who that girl was. That was the topic of my interest. But as if they conspired, the lips remained closed, nobody offered any details.

We called the cantor's wife cousin although in reality she was a cousin of my mother. I knew her and her husband way back before the war. He traveled frequently and whenever he was in our area, never missed to include us in his stops. My parents loved him. He had a beautiful voice, and my deeply religious father listened to his cantorial pieces and nostalgic Yiddish songs almost with devotion. He married our blood relative and we grew still closer to him.

Then the personal visits stopped. He settled to become the cantor and shochet who slaughtered the fowl for the households that adhered to the dietary laws. But my mother kept the relationship through frequent exchanges of letters.

By the time I paid this visit they had three children. The oldest, a girl was a mere few years younger than I. The two younger boys were handsome and sweet. I loved to watch their sand-color blond hair and the blue eyes of the youngest one that reflected an innocent child's mischievous look. I enjoyed my visit with the children and the adults. But I was preoccupied by a question. I just could not hold my questions inside me any longer. I inquired who that woman was who came to the lunch in her fur coat and fashionable skirt. My cousin told me the story that she lived with her mother and grandfather in a very small town where they returned after the deportation. Her father and the rest of the family perished. This story was not unusual. Every Jewish family had an identical story to tell. The grandfather somehow had at that time a small, but then, significant wealth. He kept an eye on the rabbi. The young lady was urged by her grandfather to get some Hebrew education, and her mother supported the idea. Her grandfather approached the rabbi to find out whether he would be willing to see his granddaughter twice a week for Hebrew lessons. The congregation did not demand his every minute so he willingly agreed. The lessons proceeded and to show appreciation for the rabbi's work, the girl's mother frequently sent some delicious home-baked pastries, some time a cake to supplement his diet, and make his lonely life somewhat sweeter. The young man was a year away from his ordination at the time of his election. His contract had a stipulation that was the general rule in the country. In order to renew the contract of rabbis who took a pulpit as bachelors and grant them life-time tenure, they had to get married before the contract year reached its end. My cousin shared with me that at one time while talking about this stipulation of his contract, the rabbi told her about an instruction one of his professor gave to the students in the Seminary, "Go out and date every eligible girl in the congregation, but marry someone from out of town." He might have looked, but did not make up his mind.

This young man became the chief rabbi not only of the local congregation but the entire mid-section of the southern part of the country, including the small town where that girl's family lived. Grandpa became interested in the life of the congregation. He frequently took the train to visit the cantor. Sometimes accompanied his granddaughter and waited for the end of her Hebrew lessons chatting with the cantor. I was also told that at one of those visits he asked the cantor and the janitor to go with him to the future home of the rabbi. There he took some measurements in the rooms and told the cantor what he thought the rabbi would need as far as furniture was concerned.

This information gave me some hints. My cousin confirmed my understanding of the situation. Grandpa wanted to make the match. He would offer some furnishings and the rabbi would ask for the hand of his granddaughter.

Relief and disappointment resulted from the conversation. On the one hand the pressure could be removed from me, but on the other hand what kind of a man was that rabbi. He most probably knew what that woman's family planned; he came with her for the noon-time lunch; escorted her to the bus station when she was ready to return home, then turned to me and asked to take a walk with him, and wanted to know whether I was willing to repeat the experience.

The two days of the holiday were uneventful. But after the holiday ended, he appeared not only for his evening meal, but asked me again to go for a walk.

I felt hurt. I really did not want to spend my time with him when the other girl was not available. I said no. He seemed to accept my word.

But as the subsequent few days witnessed it he was more persistent. On two occasions I agreed to his quest and went for a walk. I started liking him. I was impressed by him. He was young. He was well groomed. He could talk with no end in sight. He was very knowledgeable.

On the fifth day of the holiday, I got a telephone call. A member of my Zionist youth group called and in a prearranged coded message asked me to return home immediately and get ready for the move to Israel since the underground channel of escape opened. I did not have many belongings. I packed in a jiffy and ready for the train ride.

The next day the rabbi came over, and I told him very excitedly about my chance to go to Israel. He listened and his head appeared to hang somewhat lower than he usually held it. As he later told me, true to his behavior and manners with women, he offered to walk me to the train station. In a gentlemanly manner, he picked up my luggage and carried it. When we were close to the station, he stopped, turned to me, and as a lightning from the blue sky, different from his way of speaking, in a short, terse and curt sentence told me, "You have a choice. You either go to Israel, or marry me."

My answer was not much longer than his "proposal." I said, "I will go home and speak with my mother." Being merely eighteen years old, I was not accustomed to make independent decisions. I told him that. I did not know what his reaction could be to my statement.

The train arrived. I heard the words, "All aboard" and I was on the way home. I was not sure whether I could talk about this experience with my mother. I was not sure whether I wanted to. How little did I know!

When I told my mother about the proposal she handled me like I was an inexperienced, innocent little girl. She finally told me,"It is late, go to bed, we will talk about it in the morning."

This was not what I hoped to hear. The night did not provide me with a restful sleep. Thoughts were running through my mind. The proposal was exciting. There was the man who had a woman interested in him. Her family encouraged the growth of the relationship. What was in me that after six days of acquaintance he dared to propose to me? I did not think of myself as particularly pretty or beautiful, although this is what I constantly heard from friends and many adults. I had male acquaintances, I was courted. I enjoyed being in their company. In our group that signed up for the preparation to go to Israel, I met a boy whom I really liked. I can even say I fell in love with him. It was a huge decision on my part.

The morning came and went. My mother did not return to the subject. She was also undecided. Remaining true to the customs of the close-knit small Jewish community, she consulted friends and neighbors. What I overheard of their conversations was that marrying a rabbi meant entering a hard life. The rabbi is constantly in the public eye. The rabbi's wife in their own community was scrutinized very frequently even criticized. She was expected to live within the narrow boundaries that the members of the community idealized and wanted to see realized in the life of the rabbi's wife and family. The more negative comments I heard the more interesting the idea became to me.

My mother still did not talk. But somehow I found out the answer what prompted my mother to send me on the visit to the relatives rather than go home for the holiday. My sister was angry with me that I was ready to think about this marriage instead of joining her and our group to move to Israel. She told me the secret. My mother's cousin, the cantor's wife wrote my mother about the new unmarried rabbi in her community and suggested that the two of us meet.

I did not want a prearranged marriage. I saw a few in our community. This information became just one more force that added to my inner struggle with the decision. I wanted to make my decision and argued with myself that even if our meeting was prearranged, the decision was still mine. I could not arrive at a decision.

My group's aliyah was imminent. It could come any day. Meanwhile, the rabbi seemed insistent. He began writing letters. In one of his letters he inquired whether there would be any opposition to a visit to meet my family. It was not easy for my mother. She lived a life strictly defined by laws and the customs of an orthodox community. She was not sure that she could agree with the marriage of her daughter to a conservative rabbi. My mother's stand on the issue became clearer when she expressed no opposition.

He came to visit. Mother, the strict traditionalist, agreed that he could stay with us for the few days he was given by his congregation to take care of personal business. We had a pleasant time. During the day we talked and walked. My mother arranged the accommodation and to be sure that we were able to be with each other only during the days, for the night she barricaded the door to his room with a couple of chairs.

The days moved fast. He did not want to return home without hearing my decision. But it was still not made.

He left most probably disappointed, but his letters continued coming, one-a-day like the vitamin tablets which many of the children took. The letters strengthened me to make a decision when I saw that also my mother and oldest sister were in favor of the man. His letters started sounding romantic. I was swept off my feet. Although remaining true to my hard-to-get style of behavior, I said 'yes.'

Time moved as fast as the days of his visit. The decision was made that a month after our initial meeting we would have our engagement.

The engagement was to be in my hometown with no big party in the presence of just the small family circle. The financial situation of my family after the war and following my father's death did not allow great expenses. It was just a more-than-usual elaborate dinner with delicious food with all the required ceremonies and rituals.

The Zionist group left, my sister and I remained. My two brothers already left and were out of the country, my older sister was married and lived in the same city with her husband where my mother had her home.

I did not know then, but the arrangements made at that time cast a shadow on a long stretch of my life.

When we came to America, I learned a joke. In my life it was not a joke, it was reality. When a couple was ready to buy a car, the man made the decision about the make, the model, the horsepower, the extras, and the woman was gratuitously asked what color car she preferred.

Two months after our pre-arranged meeting we went to the city hall of my community and signed the binding commitment.

THE ENGAGEMENT RING

***

After our first visit in her home Ann returned to the hospital and continued her nursing education. The hospital was in the capital city. I lived about 300 kilometers south of there. Congregational duties, visitations, traveling in my district to supervise assistants and lay workers kept me close to home, the distance was too large to get away for short visits. Somehow I was able to take two days in the middle of a week. Lodging was not an issue. My married brother and my father lived in the capital city. But to find the time when Ann was off duty was an issue. She was able to get off one afternoon. I went to see her and asked whether she was willing to go downtown. She seemed agreeable. At that time I was ready to think of some wedding preparations.

We walked the streets. I was talking. I described my connections with carpenters, furniture makers and other craftsmen who could be used to fashion our future home. I really did not reveal what my plans were for that present day.

It was not aimless strolling. While walking, I knew where I wanted to take her. As it happened, I asked her to stop and look at some jewelry in the window of a store. There were earrings, pendants, necklaces, watches, and rings.

She looked and looked and said that it was an experience similar to a child let loose in a toy store. She also said that she never had a ring. When they were taken to the brick factory just before their deportation whatever valuable was on them the guards confiscated, some saying that they took the valuables for safe keeping. They were never seen again. She was fascinated by the glitter of gold and diamonds. She pointed out a few beautiful pieces which she liked. I stood by her side and waited for her to point at a ring which she really liked. I was waiting because I already had an idea what kind of engagement ring I wanted to buy for her. After a while I invited her into the store. I asked for the owner, who was an acquaintance of mine, to show us some rings. He knew what style I was interested in. I again just stood by and let the owner talk. He sounded convincing about one particular style and one specific ring. It was good salesmanship. Ann said that she liked the piece that I hoped she would choose.

I did not hesitate too long. I purchased the ring. I gently put it on her finger. Her face lit up as if all the lights, all the diamonds in the large store shined on her. I whispered in her ears that at that point we were an engaged couple. We knew that there would be no elaborate engagement party. It was too costly and impossible to host all those whom we considered close to us. All that did not matter.

We had no cars. Taxis were expensive. I did not want us to take the long walk back to her place. We just hopped on the street car. Two young people, happy. We were thinking of our present. We joked and laughed all the way back on the open end of the coach, it being the best transportation we could afford.

It was many years later in our future when Ann awakened to the realities of the world around her and realized that she had a right to make decisions, to make real choices, that she could say no. She followed my lead. It was out of love and an outcome of her upbringing and the religious teaching. It came from the motto her mother taught her when she talked about marriage. She was guided by the advice, "if you want to keep your marriage, wear a wide apron. If you do not like something, cover it by the apron."

Probably for the first time, I kissed her. Ann went to her great uncle's home, I went to my brother's. As I later learned from her, the days that followed were days of smiles and laughter for her. She did not mind going to the hospital and work the long hours required as part of her training.

I took the train and returned to my congregation. There was no day when I did not write a letter. There were some when no letter was received. The topics varied from the serious to the silly to the romantic.

During the day I was busy with the many facets of congregational work. At night, I frequently sat in the garden and watched the stars. I was wondering what she was doing. I wondered if she was gazing at the same stars and found the connection with me through those heavenly bodies. I did not know then that just a few decades later man-made stars would be orbiting the earth and electronic marvels make connection between hearts that longed for each other. These thoughts were written in my letters on the days that followed those star-gazing nights.

There were other more mundane topics to write about. Almost as a routine without any specific consideration I followed the instruction and the model I saw in the home where I grew up. My father was the decision maker and my mother the executor. I conducted negotiations, I signed contracts, I instructed workmen to prepare our home for us the new couple.

With an overgrown ego and with pride I described in my letters the color of the paint I decided for each room in the house. Detailed descriptions followed about the shape of the custom-made furniture, the list of household items I bought and prepared to put in the future pantry and the cupboards. I was writing with great enthusiasm.

The replies puzzled me. Rather the lack of replies. They just repeated some of the items I wrote in my letters like recounting those statements. Although these lines puzzled me, I was not thinking seriously that there was anything behind Ann's lack of enthusiastic interest. I knew that I did what a caring man was supposed to do for his future bride and, even farther into the future, for his family. I was to become a husband, a provider. I thought I could plan and do everything with authority as I was acting in my rabbinic roles.

Ann was a very young girl when she was uprooted by the family's deportation. Not a full year after their return from deportation, her father died of an illness he contracted in the concentration camp. Her brothers moved out of the house. They were preparing for their escape and underground move to Palestine. For her a real adult male role model was not available. She told me after many years of marriage that she accepted my behavior, although she was deeply hurt in her world of emotions. She was not taught that she had a right to speak up. She did not dare to think that her opinion was important enough to be expressed about the shape of her future home. She was waiting for an invitation to have input into these decisions. Since they were not forthcoming, she went along with my decisions without real enthusiasm, keeping the hurt hidden behind the 'big apron'. The hidden hurt turned into a shadow of the pulpit under which she lived for numerous years of her life.

THE WEDDING

The days between the engagement and the wedding moved slowly. My desire to see Joel made the time seem to pass sluggishly. The daily letters came, and a large part of my days was spent by reading and rereading them.

The wedding plans had been formulated already at our engagement dinner. It was understood that the state required civic marriage would be in my city. In his congregation there was no possibility to have another rabbi come to officiate. His father's congregation was served by a rabbi who was a graduate of the same Seminary, and they already had an established friendship. He wanted to have also a close friend from his early childhood to be part of the wedding ceremony along with one of his professors. My family was to host the dinner in the only kosher establishment in the city.

He took a few personal days again and came to my hometown. We signed our civic wedding certificate at City Hall. According to the law we were married. But not according to our belief and religious law. Walking home, my sister made it harder for us. Innuendoes and not so discrete suggestions were made that we were married and we can go to their apartment and enjoy a time of privacy in seclusion. I was married, he was married, and we remained separated. Following some religious tradition, we did not see each other until the wedding in the synagogue.

The next day he had to return to his congregation. Before he left, he told me in his sheepish way how awkward it was for him to return to his home as a married man and not introduce his wife to his congregants.

I was not less excited and tortured by agonizing thoughts than any other bride. But as I recall the number of thoughts about the man whom

I was to marry was larger than the thoughts about myself. I was wondering about him. What I did not know was that he had to face hard times.

Almost two more weeks passed before we became married in all aspects of our life. Those days held several tasks to perform. He grew up respecting and following his father's teachings. He was raised to live by the principle that a man undertakes a task only if he had accomplished the goal that preceded it. It meant to him that he had to complete his education before he would get married. According to his father's principle he had to take his final examinations before he got married. As it turned out, he completed his examinations on Monday, and our wedding was on the following day, Tuesday.

There was another pressing circumstance. He was not yet ordained as rabbi when he was elected by his congregation. Following an unwritten convention, rabbis of that country had to be married men. He had been serving already eight months when he set his eyes on me. His contract stated that in order to keep his position, he was to marry within a year. It just happened that he was in the right place at the right time when I appeared on the scene. His contract agreement might have put pressure on him, but even if at times I was not sure of myself, two things were clear to me. Had he not liked me and had he not fallen in love with me, he would have not asked me to marry him. The other point I was sure of was that he did not marry me for my money, expecting a huge dowry. I had no money, no inheritance, no dowry.

My family members gathered in the home of my great-uncle in the opposite part of the city from where our wedding was to take place and with great excitement prepared for the wedding.

Unbeknown to me, the excitement of my fiancee was not as clear as ours. As it happened his father favored another woman. He wished he married her since he grew up in the same area of the country where that woman's family came from and already had a kind of acquaintance with them. At that time I did not know that a half-an-hour before its starting time his father suggested that he go not to the wedding. I did not know about it, yet it was a relief to see him walk down the aisle in the synagogue.

The events of World War II reduced the size of our wedding party. On my side my sisters, a brother-in-law, and four members on my father's side were present. His family was truncated, too. His mother perished in the Holocaust; his father, brother and his spouse returned from the camps; his grandmother, an uncle, and aunt with their spouses survived and lived in the city. They were in attendance. Some of his invited friends shared the dinner table with us.

The wedding dinner took too long for my expectation. But I learned then and later that when three rabbis are given the chance to speak at the simchah of one of their colleagues, they do not pay much attention to the hands of the clock.

The speeches were beautiful and long. They heaped compliment after compliment upon the young rabbi. The few words they spared for me sounded like their well-intended suggestions how I should and would fulfill the duties of the rabbi's wife and meet the expectations of his congregation. That old friend, the candidate who applied for the pulpit and did not get elected, spoke of the truly personal aspects of their friendship. They knew each other inside and out. They were friends already for many years and remained such for many more, although the friend married and moved to Israel.

Although my wedding dress was not imported from Paris or New York, I still cherished it. It was my wedding gown made by my mother and a seamstress. I liked it even if it reminded me of one of the outfits I sewed for my doll. I had my plans. It was simple and practical. It was a two-piece garment. I wanted to shorten the skirt after the wedding and have a beautiful summer suit to wear.

My groom appeared very dignified. He wore his brocade robe with a wide velvet collar, fashioned after the Hungarian noble mens' a few centuries before. His head was covered with the six-sided miter-like headgear made of the same material as the robe. One could have taken him for a priest in his best if the hat was not made six-pointed, a reminder of the six points of the Star of David, and not the priests' four-sided ones fashioned after the four points of the cross.

The late June air was hot and stifling even in that early evening hour. Finally the glass had been broken, permission was given to kiss the bride, we were pronounced husband and wife. We greeted the well-wishers and, since there were no Cadillacs or limousines, we stepped up into a flower-decorated fiacre, the small hackney coach that waited for us to take us to the photographer's studio.

Whether the photographer was funny or not, it was good to have a few laughs as he moved us as mannequins just to get poses he considered appropriate. We really could hardly wait to get into a more relaxed mode.

It came when we entered the small dining hall. The room still wore the signs of the war which ended merely four years before.

The dinner menu was simple and the food delicious. We really did not notice it. The excitement and being the center of attention blocked our taste buds. But everyone said so. We had to believe it.

The rabbis who were also our wedding guests remained true to their training. Unlike those in America, no one dared to say, "Rabbi, make it short." They did not learn it on their own, either. The series of speeches continued. It was the custom to discuss some religious subject, or present something inspirational in the disguise of being humorous. The atmosphere turned serious when the groom was to deliver his discourse. He shined as he showed his training and education. Using the formats of Talmudic discourses, he derived meaning from the numerical value of the Hebrew letters that formed the date of the wedding and the new bride's name.

Listening to those speeches but not allowing the words to sink in I was touched at a vulnerable spot deep inside me. I heard the presentation of learned man. They formulated their thoughts in poetic prose and crystal clear sentences. I was fearful not knowing how I would measure up to these people in the environment they represented to me. My attention span proved inadequate to integrate all that was said about the virtues of the rabbi's wife in her responsible position of handling the intricate ways of congregational life. My education did not come close to theirs. Lack of finances, lack of opportunities, and the consequences of the anti-Jewish laws, deportation, and ruined dreams did not give me a chance. In my daydreaming I thought of the wives of the few rabbis whom I knew. They either came from rich families or were university graduates. I questioned myself and sat with my trembling heart and mind. My thoughts reached the shadow which I created as my alter ego. I felt small to the task. I doubted that I would be able to live up to the requirements of the field which I just entered. A shadow seemed to expand around me. It was the shadow of the shining, bright, rabbinic home and position that hung all around me. I wanted to be left alone, together with my new husband and look forward to the future which I just entered.

As the guests left, and we prepared to move to the hotel where we stayed overnight, I came to see the man, whom I married, and his vocation in a different light. In my youthful thinking I did not deal with these heavy issues when the excitement of becoming a wife fully occupied my emotional world.

A Strange World

My husband completed his education, took his final exams in the summer of 1949 on a Monday. We got married following a traditional Jewish way. Tuesday was chosen for our wedding day, based on the biblical creation story. There it is said that God saw all that He created on the third day, and twice expressed His satisfaction, stating that it was good. Tradition holds that Tuesday is a good and blessed day.

Right after our wedding I learned that Joel's life and mine were very different. The students of the Rabbinical School spent twelve–and a–half years together in the same school. Their social life was in a great part connected. It was as if they communicated in sign language. They understood their short references to events of their lives, to their memories. They shared inside jokes.

My husband spent more than his hours in school with his very close friend. They shared their private lives, too. A newcomer could be easily intimidated by their closeness and feel strange and excluded in their company. Joel did not find objectionable that his friend and his wife took their vacation at the same time and place where we were to spend the first week of our married life. It was so natural to them that they did not inform me about this arrangement in advance. I found it out on the train that took us to the vacation villa owned by the central organization of the country's Jewry. All rabbis were given time to take their vacation at that place. It was not that we went there because my husband was cheap; it was the custom. It was easier to follow an old custom than to break new grounds.

My expectations were different. I longed for privacy away from the shadow that I felt overcoming me in the presence of his colleagues and their wives from the very beginning when I first met them. I did not like the intrusion the friend and his wife represented.

Maybe denial, maybe the beauty of the natural setting had an effect on me. The colors of early summer, the mountains, and the lake's smooth surface calmed my inner confusion. Although the meals of the day were served in the dining room, we had time to be alone, just the two of us. The walks around the lake, through the narrow paths between the trees evoked the memories of our strolls during the nights and evenings at the beginning of our acquaintance. But my husband expressed his concern. He did not have any way to relate to my quiet, almost total withdrawal. I was not showing my social graces. I preferred solitude over the mingling with the other rabbis and their wives.

The first morning there I wished not to have breakfast in the dining room. I wanted to show what a caring wife I was. I knew already from the short two months between our meeting and marriage that my husband liked chocolate milk. I was eager to please him, I set the small table in the room and let him sit like a king who is catered to by his queen. I put the cups on the table, chocolate milk all prepared. He silently offered his few words of blessing before partaking a meal and began his breakfast. I did not feel hungry. I just sat and waited for his reaction. He dutifully drank the breakfast beverage the same way he learned in his home and in the dining halls of the schools. He was prepared "to finish up the plate, or in this case the cup, to the last drop."

I changed my mind. Instead of looking at myself just as a waitress or maid, I sat with him at the table. I poured a cup of the chocolate drink for myself. I took just one sip, and screamed, "stop." I realized from the taste and flavor that my desire to please was stronger that my culinary expertise. Instead of sugar, I had poured salt in the mixture.

He did not say a word. I don't know what he thought of the meals I was to serve in the future. His facial expression did not reveal his thoughts, but I was delighted to see that he forgave my mistake and hoped that he would be this kind about my mistakes in the future, too.

After our honeymoon we did not move directly in our new home. We had to make a stop before. A great day was still ahead of us. The ordination of the two new rabbis, my husband and only one of his classmates.

Before the war my husband's class was the largest in the Seminary's history. After having survived the German occupation and the Holocaust only two decided to continue their studies and become ordained as rabbis.

The Seminary's synagogue was festively set for the occasion. I was honored as the wife of one who was being ordained. I had to overcome my shyness and accept the reserved seat in the first row of the pews.

The professors, the members of the examining board, and the signees of the Semichah opened the academic procession, then came the two.

Later in our lives I heard about the intricacies of the ordination program. The seminary curriculum offered a twelve-and-a-half year program that began with the higher grades of high school studies. Secular and sacred subjects were taught in full-day instruction six days a week. At the senior year in the high school department the students already looked ahead at the future and the bargaining began. An agreement was reached in my husband's class one year before the German occupation that at the ordination he would deliver the vernacular reply to the rector's ordination speech while another classmate would speak in Hebrew. By the time of the ordination that student already lived in Israel, and since only two finished the required studies, by the nature of events the second ordained had the honor of delivering the Hebrew address.

I was tense. I listened. In his speech my husband used a verse, read in the synagogues as part of that week's prophetic lesson, to outline the goal of his service to congregations. I could not truly appreciate all he planned to do, but it was clear to me that he decided to serve the common people, care for the needy, and made a clear commitment that he would not serve a congregation larger than 365 families, corresponding to the number of days in a year—in his interpretation—to devote at least one day a year to each member family. His dream was to get thoroughly acquainted with every member. He wanted to know the past history, live the present, and be as much as possible part of forming and shaping the future of every family.

The glorious day was over, but even then dark clouds gathered on the horizon. Our joy was mixed with a feeling of shock and sadness. The rabbi of the synagogue who officiated at our wedding suddenly without any warning sign died at a young age and we were to attend his funeral. It was with a heavy heart that we headed to our new home.

The thoughts that occurred to me after I had served the first breakfast on our honeymoon popped up frequently in the early years of our marriage. When it came to the quality of meals, I prepared, I needed his empathetic understanding and forgiveness.

My soups were so thick that we could make the spoon stand in them straight and upright. My pasta was over cooked, the Sabbath cholent was either dried out or too soupy. But I could not count on my husband's help or input. Although his mother taught him to mend socks, sew on bottons, and do some cross stitches, in true Hungarian tradition the man of the house would not immerse his hand in the water to wash the dishes. Because that was considered sacrilegious, he would not have learned the process that preceded dishwashing, to prepare even the simplest meal.

There was a quid-pro-quo. In truth I would not have thought of breaking even this kind of secular tradition asking for his assistance in kitchen matters. But throughout my life I considered myself a true enemy of the sewing needle. My husband used the skills he learned from his mother, he took care of missing bottons and made some mending when it was needed. He also proved himself to be good in performing some smaller tasks around the house that he learned from his father. He became the handyman for the entire family. He did the odd jobs not only in our home, but in my mother's, too. Each time before we visited her, she called and asked him to take along his tool box.

I was young. I was more interested in living than slaving in my mother's kitchen or perfect my sewing details. I had no experience. But my mother was helpful. Every week two or three recipes, with detailed instructions how to use them, were enclosed in her letters to make my meals more palatable.

New Experiences

On the way home after the ordination I was full of expectations. As the new bride who was to begin her married life, my inner eyes focused on every room of the house that was to become our home. I pictured every piece of furniture. I even had an idea what was where since during our courting days my future husband informed me about his accomplishments step by step in his letters. I knew the shape and color of every nick-knack. I knew all about the bedding that he had custom made. Thinking of my home I had some creepy feelings around my stomach, but I did not know until much later what it was.

It was wonderful that I was led into a fully furnished house, but I did not feel that it was my home. I had no input into the process that would have made it my home, or our home. I lived in the shadow.

When we settled into our everyday routine, my husband talked to me about his plans. He wanted to show his pride in his new wife and planned to introduce me to every family in the congregation. The mornings he spent in the chapel and the office. In the afternoons he taught the very few children and some adults who wanted to learn. The evenings were the time to visit the members.

My husband came from a family where alcoholic drinks were not part of the menu. In the small community where kosher households were not the rule, the hosts wanted to be hospitable to us. The only way to host the rabbi and his wife was to offer some liquor or cordials. I was not used to drinking either, but there was no way to refuse.

Some of these visits were pleasant, some unpleasant, some humorous.

One day we had an appointment with one of the better-to-do families who already established a comfortable living for themselves. I was fairly excited since this family with their financial abilities supported the congregation, and I was interested to see how they succeeded to rebuild a family life after the war.

My husband followed his principle he learned a long time before that the courtesy of a civilized person is punctuality. To him being on time up to the minute was of utmost importance. I wished to live more relaxed. I just could not imagine that arriving ten minutes late for a planned visit could mean the end of the world. I started thinking that I did not know who and what I was. In his anxieties about becoming late, my husband started asking me a half-an-hour before we were to leave whether I could be ready on time. I questioned what I was, a young child who had to be reminded of what to do and how to get ready. I questioned whether I could not be trusted to take care of myself and be aware of time. I was cautious and uncomfortable every time before we were going somewhere.

Nevertheless, at that time too, we were on time. After ringing the bell, the door opened, the male head of the household stood in front of me. He welcomed us, shook hands and introduced himself. I was speechless, I could not squeeze out one sound, my throat closed up. The name by which he introduced himself was not familiar. Their last name was not one of the usual German family names, which the Jews were forced to take in the 1770s under the Habsburg rule. I did not recognize the name, but I recognized the face. It was a frightening flashback. I saw that face. I saw that face frequently. But then he did not wear the tailored custom-made suit of fine imported woollen fabric. That face brought back the image of the Kapo in the concentration camp. He was the one to whom my mother went begging for some medicine and food for my deadly ill father. I cannot describe in detail how he treated my mother and how cruelly he refused any intervention or help. I stood there. I shook his hand, but I could not look into his face, I could not utter a sound.

Other visits offered other experiences. We called upon the family who lived around the corner from us in the early days of December. As we turned the corner, I saw their four or five year old son who hurried from the street into the yard of their house. Meanwhile we came closer to the gate when I heard the boy yelling from the top of his lung, "Dad, close the gate, the Rabbi is coming."

Early December was the time when the general population killed the hog that provided the fat and the meat for the entire family for the whole coming year. That Jewish family did not need the services of the shochet (ritual slaughterer) who killed the chickens and geese for those who observed the Jewish dietary laws. They slaughtered their pig which observant Jews would not do since biblical law forbade all uses of pork and pork products.

The visits with congregational families took up almost all of our evenings. During the days I had a considerable amount of time on my hands. I had live-in help. There was just so much I could read. I could not even think of doing work outside the house although I was used to working. I worked in the hospital six days a week. During the short acquaintance with each other, on one occasion I asked my fiancee what his opinion was about me working after we got married. I understood that he said something that sounded like an agreement. But at the time I broached the subject again, my husband quite sternly and vehemently expressed his opinion that he changed his mind about it. He thought about this subject, looked at what the wives of his colleagues were doing, and he arrived at the conclusion that it was not proper for the rabbi's wife to take on any job. He even assured me that there would be numerous activities in the life of the congregation where I could work and would be expected to participate. All these activities would take up the time which I found idle non-productive periods during the day.

It was a promise, but it was still in the future. I found myself unfulfilled and frequently bored. Two months into our marriage, I called my younger sister and asked her to come and spend some time with me. Although newlyweds, shortly after our wedding we became a three-person household. I enjoyed her company. Her presence carried with it a taste of my home. The weekdays were easy. We did some housework together, we talked, and laughed. Our conversations flowed seemingly endlessly.

Saturday mornings were of a different story. My husband spent long hours at services which women did not usually attend. The two of us were left alone at home. The live-in help took off and frequently went to her family on Saturdays and Sundays.

The families whom we visited somehow were satisfied that they could host the rabbi and his wife by offering some "liquid refreshment." When it came to repay our visits, or on occasions when they wanted to do something for the newlyweds, usually brought or had some good liquor delivered to the house. We set up a liquor cabinet and in no time we had a considerable collection.

On one of those long Saturday mornings my sister and I decided to taste some of the liquors. We did not know much about their strength, alcohol content, sweetness, or flavoring. Whatever name on the bottle sounded interesting or strange, we filled our shot glasses from the content and enjoyed ourselves. It was too much of a good thing. We did not know what happened to us until the knocks on the window panes woke us up from our sleep on the floor. My husband came home from services. He did not carry a key to the house on Saturday, one of us had to get up and open the gate. I never knew before what a difficult job it was to find a key, put it in the lock, and open a door. Interestingly enough he did not ask what happened. I opened the door. He looked at me, walked into the house, saw the other door, that of the liquor cabinet, and it was clear to him what entertainment the two young mischievous ladies provided for themselves. While he was offering fervent prayers in the temple, they took a libation of the fermented substances. As if we were confessing sins committed in relation to another human being which our Day of Atonement (Yom Kippur) could not undo, we vowed that for a long time we would not partake any of the heavenly nectar. The decision proved to be the right one.

Joel was a few years older than I. As a new husband, he was eager to become a new father. I became aware that he was preoccupied with a question whether all was well with me or probably with us that in the first two months I did not become pregnant. He looked at me with questioning eyes, he inquired about my family history. He wanted to know the number of children my mother and my grandmothers had. Soon I provided the answer. Eleven months into our marriage our first born arrived.

There was no more inquiry whether I could take a job. The now three-member family filled up my days. There was always something to do. I did not miss my training and my work in the hospital. I worked more than six days. My job became a seven-day-a-week, twenty-four-hour-a-day full-time occupation. The live-in help came very handy, and what I most enjoyed, my mother came to spend time with us. I did not need the two recipes a week in her letters. She cooked and baked. She was well trained in the care of new babies. I was more than just the rabbi's wife, I became the mother of our child.

THE MOVE

The birth of our son was one of the happiest moments in my life. But this event taught me something about my husband, about his attitude, and about his idea of being a rabbi and a family man.

Before he decided to accept the position in the congregation where we met and our son was born, he expressed his desire at the Central Bureau of Hungarian Jews and the Secretary of the Rabbinical Association to apply to a congregation that was larger and offered more cultural and social activities.

A congregation was interested in his candidacy and several weeks before the birth of our son my husband was called and arranged to travel for an interview and introductory weekend so the members would have an opportunity to decide whether he was acceptable to them.

The plan was made. My husband firmly believed that once an agreement was made, it could not be broken. One hour after I gave birth, with a heavy heart he said so long and left for the interview. Although he called upon arrival and every day after, I felt abandoned, lonely, and above all not cared about.

The joy of the birth of our son was overshadowed by the commitments my husband made to his calling and profession. His decision and act cast the long dark shadow on my thoughts about my future. My fear was that I would live my entire life in the shadow of the pulpit. I feared that if that most important event, the birth of our child could not break his devotion, probably less significant duties will be valued more than the sensitivities of the family.

The interview took place, he liked the congregation. The board seemed to be pleased with his approach to their needs. But politics and the decision makers' personal interests interfered, and behind the scenes they recommended the election of another young rabbi. He represented some danger to the national leadership through his connection with the communist party, and they wanted him to be away from the center of Jewish activities. The congregation gave in to the pressure, and that man was elected.

The plan did not work out. Through his connections, that rabbi could refuse to move to the city where he was elected and fill the rabbinic position with week end visits. The other days he was able to spend with his family in the capital city. The national leaders then turned into a different direction. They demanded that he move there. He refused. Subsequently he lost all his chances to continue a rabbinic career in Hungary. The officials then saw it fit to fill the position with the rabbi who was ordained with my husband. But one year later this rabbi along with some others, including us, was given the opportunity to leave for the new State of Israel.

We agreed to try again. The rabbinic position which my husband already interviewed before, opened up again. Another trial resulted in a contract with lifetime tenure. When our son was one year old, we moved. My husband became the chief rabbi of a much larger district of the country with more and difficult tasks to perform. The question burned inside me again. More responsibilities, less time for the family. How will I adjust to that?

THE SYSTEM

The 1948 election held at the point of Soviet bayonets changed the climate and the euphoria that expected democratic institutions after World War II. The Soviet Union dramatically and forcefully molded the political system into its own image.

The local authorities had the power to decide on restrictions on their own. One of the serious effects on our lives was when rations were introduced and the local officials decided what and how much was given to the citizens. As a clergy, my family and I were not entitled to the usual sugar, flower, butter, and margarine rations. That we had a baby was not taken into consideration. I was helpless and angry. Maybe my anger influenced me to save the official notification about that decision. Somehow I hoped that one day I will be able to attest to that injustice. By sheer accident it was part of the content of the luggage which Ann took as baby's belongings and we still have it.

Like all clergy in the country, I was required to take loyalty vows in the presence of the local mayor and party representative or the officials of the reorganized Ministry of Religious Affairs. The atmosphere of the monthly Rabbinical Association meetings fell under outside control. One of our gatherings was attended by a colleague in his captain's uniform. At that time he served as chaplain in the army. He sat with us and later requested the floor. He outlined what the rabbis' duty was in the People's Republic. In short, he stated that, in order to promote the welfare of the state and to demonstrate our loyalty to the regime, rabbis had to teach the ideology of socialism and communism in our theological language. Referring to our liturgical duties, he announced that from that day on our daily prayer book had to be the teaching of the Moscow installed national leader

Matthew Rakosi, and for the festival prayer book we were to use the teachings that Stalin pronounced for the benefit of world proletariat.

Although I did not join any political party, my thinking was closest to the democrats'. That ideology did not go well with the request our chaplain colleague outlined. Subsequently at the close of the meeting I went to the president of our association and the president of National Office of Jewish Congregations to announce that I decided to resign from the rabbinate. I was shocked to hear the reply that I had to remain in my position as long as the reigns were in the hands of our national leaders. They could not allow me to resign because the West would use my decision for propaganda purposes and feed the news media, printed or otherwise, with the information that in our country there was no religious freedom.

Our "freedom" had been demonstrated in many different forms. The government of that era wanted the world to believe that there was religious freedom in the country. The airwaves were used to provide a facade toward achieving this goal. Each month one of the country's rabbis was given the task to deliver a radio sermon in the framework of a half-an-hour religious programming. The sermon had to be submitted three weeks in advance to be censored. The first time it was my term, at the gate of the studio, the uniformed police greeted and ordered me to follow him. When I entered the studio itself, I was puzzled. Directly opposite to the microphone there was an elevated glass cage. Minutes before the beginning of the program, a man entered the enclosure with some sheets of paper. Later I found out that it was a copy of my sermon and he checked every letter, word, and sentence whether I would attempt to delineate from the text. In one sentence I made a mistake and misread a word. The man in the cage shook his closed fist at me in a threatening manner.

Another way demonstrated our freedom In both congregations whose rabbi I was, there were men who faithfully attended the services. It was pleasing to me, the Rabbi. Not all members showed that kind of devotion. One man showed a greater interest than others. Somehow he befriended me, and established a good relationship with me. It was many years later that I learned about his devotion. It was not to the congregation. He was the built-in spy to report the people who attended services, my behavior, thinking, and political orientation, and specifically the topic of my sermons.

One year, immediately after the fall holidays, I was directed to appear in the central office of the Jewish Administrative board. That was the time when legal and illegal immigrants arrived to the newly established State of Israel. Due to the lack of better housing they were housed in tents of aluminum sheets and cardboard. At the end of one service on the Festival of Tabernacles (Sukkot), I asked for the blessing of peace on all who lived under the protection of tents.

I was called to hear that I entered forbidden territories and in those closing words I spread illegal Zionist propaganda.

The person who faithfully attended services in my second congregation was none else than the president. He was an excellent locksmith. In the turmoil that followed the 1956 uprising, someone discovered a list of secret police agents. The president's name was among them. In the role of double-agent he played a significant role in my life. Having been captured close to the Austrian border and undergone a change in the original sentence delivered by the military court, on route to the Siberian labor camp, among hundreds of other captives, I was locked up in the prison of my city that before the uprising was run by the dreaded secret security service. The president was instrumental in my kidnaping from that prison then under Russian administration.

Any joy that we experienced under the oppressive regime was overshadowed by the daily fear. Religious education on paper was allowed in public schools, but such restrictions surrounded that permission that in practice there could not be any religious course given. One of the requirements was that in order to hold religious classes in every grade there had to be twenty students of the same denomination who requested the subject. In many communities the total number of Jewish students was under that number. These circumstances required me to travel four days a week and teach underground every time in a different student's home.

One December night while returning from my visits to the different communities that belonged to our district, the train on which I traveled stopped at one of the stations and for some reason delayed its departure. Suddenly armed soldiers, civilian detectives entered each coach and began examining our internal passports and identification papers. When they came to me and saw my papers, I was ordered to detrain. I was escorted to a narrow cell at the station in which it was impossible to turn from one side to the other. I became anxious because I worried that my wife expected me to be home at a certain time, and I was held prisoner in a cell about twenty kilometers from our home.

There was no interrogation, they did not demand any information even when the door was opened and allowed me to return to the train. Watching the people who were returning with me, I saw a number of nuns. That was the night when Cardinal Joseph Mindszenty was arrested. For security reasons any clergy who was "loose" at that time was taken into custody.

Back at home, that evening a popular joke ran through my mind several times. In a communist country happiness was hearing the door bell, opening the door, and being informed that the wanted person lived in the next apartment.

GATHERING CLOUDS

The executive orders which directed many aspects of our daily lives, made stability and security a far cry in our every-day reality. An ever-present fear clouded our future. The political system did not honor our right to privacy either as a family or a family of which one member had his professional office in that home.

There was a shortage of housing. A register was maintained about the size of homes. Those that were larger than allowed by the department of housing were ordered to accept others to share the living space. Our home fell into this category. We faced the dilemma. We had a choice, to take a family, assigned by the authorities, into our home, or to find people who were in need in housing, and, at the same time, seemed trustworthy. It was difficult to trust anybody in a country where everyone was under suspicion of being a spy who reported to the authorities. In our search for a solution we learned that a young Jewish man was to be transferred from his job to fill a position in our city. We invited him, and he moved in. Later when he was transferred, two women shared our living space. When they moved and we were left without a boarder, the sister of the young man who was transferred came to our city and took her brother's room as her residence. She resided with us up to the time of the uprising.

Not knowing for certain what we could expect from those with whom we were forced to share our home, other doubts crept into our mind and fears into our hearts.

When I was awakened with the rambling of truck tires, or when it sounded like a truck stopped in the vicinity of our home, immediately a terror came over my entire being that my husband might have been involved in an activity which the authorities judged hostile to the regime, or someone accused him with making some anti-government statement, and it was his turn to be taken away from us.

The north end of the building complex, the home of the defunct religious school, opposite to the rabbi's home, the temple's office, and the residence of the cantor, was occupied by school age children who were kidnaped from Greece and brought to Hungary to receive their communist education. The temple was built between these two wings attached to them, forming a U shape. We were aware that those children were instructed to keep an eye on what was going on in the two other buildings.

The insecurity that we felt every hour in our life cast a shadow from the present to the future.

We had two children. The time fast approached that our son would have reached school age. The years in elementary school would have meant ideological indoctrination, joining the youth group, wearing the uniform of the young communist " Ground breakers."

Beyond elementary school the chances for a higher education seemed to become increasingly slimmer. Children of clergy were branded as coming from families which were officially held as enemies of the working class. We valued education very highly, and it pained me to think no matter how smart, talented, or advanced my children would grow, their chances to be accepted to a university were either very limited or nil. The thought burnt in me literally during the day and sleepless nights.

Our son entered first grade. I was crying when I took him to register in the school of our district. He was an exceptional child. (Which mother would not say that about her son?). I cried when I thought of the limitations his future might have held for him.

While waiting in line, I remembered an incident which happened during one of our vacations in the villa on the lake with some of the other rabbis. He was two years old. One time at the dinner table he had a sheet of paper in front of him and was drawing. One of the senior rabbi's wife passed behind him. While doodling and writing some letters, he amused himself by singing the songs I taught him. The older lady stopped, listened, looked at the paper, and asked him about the letters he wrote. He named every one of them correctly. She turned to me, blocked her mouth with her palm and whispered into my ears, "Don't tell anybody how old he is. Someone may cast an evil eye on him." Inside, I smiled. I knew how smart he was. I did not believe in the evil eye, but outwardly I cried because I feared for his and his sister's future.

He went to school. He loved it. Every day he came home and with great excitement told me what he learned in school.

At that time, during the Stalin era, it was forbidden to sing Hebrew or Yiddish songs in public. I frequently sang the song about the Messiah coming. I did not believe in old-wives tales and was not sure about the coming of the Messiah in our life time or any other in the near future. Despite my lack of belief, something similar to the coming of a redeemer happened.

One October morning, following my daily routine, I went to the open farmers' market early. I bought what we needed and on the way home somebody stopped me and asked whether I heard that the young people in the capital city stormed the radio station, and the secret police fired live ammunition at them. They still succeeded in taking over the radio and reading a declaration containing their demands. The demonstrators moved to Heroes Square and few of them climbed the base of Stalin's statue and succeeded toppling it.

My steps became faster and faster as I was eager to reach my home. Before I turned on the radio I stepped in the bedroom where my husband was still sleeping. Hurriedly I woke him up and told him what I heard on the street. Then we heard the details of the night's events on the radio. At home, I went to the kitchen to start my daily chores when a boy, probably seventeen, knocked on the door and came in. His clothing looked like a poor beggar's, he was unshaven and wanted to speak with the rabbi. When I called him, Joel hurriedly dressed up and—changing his routine—before offering his morning prayer, came to the kitchen. He listened to the stranger who told him that he needed to leave the country since he was one of those who tore down Stalin's statue. He hoped that Joel, the rabbi, closest to the border could help. Joel said only a few words and asked the boy to follow him.

He remembers the details of this event. He is the one to tell what took place in their walk and afterwards.

I, the mother of two children and the wife of a man who by his vocation was not trusted by the governing bodies, feared for the lives of all of us. Revolution, uprising. I asked the question which I frequently heard from many other Jews, "Is this good for us, the Jews?" Then I did not have the answer that I know now.

RESCUE AND ESCAPE

1956

On the first day of the uprising that exhausted young man asked for my help. Being Jewish, he came to me, the rabbi whose congregation was the closest to the Austrian border, and he counted on my assistance. He told me about the beginning of the students' uprising and the demolition of Stalin's statue in a very personal manner. He had to escape since he was one of the young students who dethroned Stalin's bronze image on Heroes Square.

I did not believe the heroic story of this seventeen-year-old. But without asking any questions I told him to follow me with the intention that I would hire a taxi to take him close to the border. I had not much hope in succeeding.

Although we moved hurriedly, suddenly he left me and stepped in the small store that was on our left. He came back as fast as he went in, holding the morning paper in his hand. He showed me the front page. There was the dramatic picture of the moment when the young men climbed the base of Stalin's statue and made the first move to knock it down. Here he was, my companion, with whom I walked the streets of our city.

I did not need any other documentation. At the stand I saw my acquaintance, the taxi driver. He already knew more of the revolution than I who was just awakened and briefed in a few words. I did not have to say much. The driver understood the situation, but before I paid the fare, the young man slipped a piece of paper in my hand and said, "This is my mother's telephone number; please, notify her as soon as you heard from the driver that I escaped."

I returned home worried about his safety and life.

The radio was our constant source of information against the many rumors that were spread. Under the circumstances there was no way to check the validity of the news. The news was good in the first four days. The uprising of the young generation clamored for and demanded a change from the Moscow-directed dictatorship to a national communist system similar to Tito's Yugoslavia. Not being members of the party, we did not occupy leadership positions of the oppressive system. We welcomed the efforts. It did not make much difference whether we were Jews and non-Jews, where we stood politically. But the fifth day began to show a different picture. One of the parish priests in our city introduced the religious issue. Moved in the company of a crowd to City Hall Plaza, erected a huge cross and delivered a vitriolic speech questioning on which side the Jews stood.

The conditions were alarming. At night, I called a special meeting of my congregation's board of officers. After having thoroughly considered the circumstances, we asked my brother-in-law to slip through the insufficiently guarded border and seek out the Vienna rabbi who was one of my predecessors. He accepted the task and next morning returned with a considerable amount of money. The Board under the leadership of the vice-president decided to divide the money into halves. I was to deliver one half to the revolutionary council and keep the other half as a fund in case we needed to help people who had to flee. The money was accepted as the Jewish community's contribution and support of the revolution's efforts.

Bad news reached us from the eastern and northern parts of the country. Several communities reported anti-Jewish atrocities. The purity of the revolution's goal was badly stained.

It was only twelve years after the beginning of our destruction in the Holocaust. I formulated plans. With four other members of the congregation we developed our plans to find rescue channels at least for the country's Jewish children. The revolution took a toll on the nerves. We planned to organize groups of two hundred and gain permission to send them to "youth camps" in Austria allegedly for two-week periods. When the return date would come close, we planned to report that a contagious disease broke out and we were required to quarantine the children and only the adult chaperons could return to take the next group. The task of organization fell on me. I approached the Revolutionary Council for permission to travel. Recognizing the financial support I delivered there was no objection to issuing a permit.

My wife became terrorized. She talked with me at length attempting to persuade me not to travel to the capital to engage the help of the Israeli Embassy, the American Consulate, and Red Cross. On the eighth day of the revolution I got a ride on a military bus. I was able to begin the negotiations only with the Israeli consul. I was told that it would take some time, but the plan seemed to be a good one. Since the plan was put into motion I was offered a ride home in a diplomatic car on Saturday, the third of November. I did not accept the Sabbath offer and asked for the ride on Sunday morning. I was given the unpublished home number of the consul. My nerve-wrecking waiting began. There was periodic turmoil on the streets. Shortages of food became a daily problem. One day, I had to stand in cue to wait for some bread distribution. While waiting in front of the store, from somewhere a rocket hit the street. A few of us fell to the ground. The signs were not promising. There was no long-distance telephone service, messages were disseminated over the radio to families whose member was in a different community. I dispatched four messages hoping that my family would get some signs of life from me.

The days passed at a snail's pace. Early Sunday morning when my return home was planned, I called the consul. He delivered the bad news. The Russian troops returned, occupied the roads, even diplomatic traffic was not allowed. Fate made me the prisoner of circumstances.

Five days later, I received a note from the vice-president of the congregation. He came on a truck that delivered food supplies from the rural areas to the capital city. He saw a chance for me to return home and named the place and time where I was to report for the ride. I had to be there before noon. The streets were filled with Russian soldiers, some policing the streets, some lying dead on the streets, burned when their trucks were attacked with Molotov cocktails. I reached the destination. I climbed in the back of the truck. The canvas was lowered. The vice-president was there, positioned himself close to me so the others on the truck would not hear his words and whispered in my ears. "You will not find your family at home." Not one more word. The whole ride was a misery. I did not know the meaning of the few words. Where was my family? Were they arrested because of my activities? Were they imprisoned? Had the authorities moved them? Did anyone have any information about where they were?

Every time the truck was stopped on the road for checking the passengers, I trembled that they were looking for me. Finally we arrived. The president and I took to the road home. We lived in the same vicinity. He then told me that a large number of our congregation left for Austria as soon as the border guards withdrew and it was possible to cross over. Among the escapees were my wife, her mother, sisters, brothers-in-law, their three children and our two. But there was no further information about them to anybody's knowledge.

The news was devastating. I felt so alone. The majority of the congregation left. The Temple building stood a silent witness to two destructions of the once noble and respected congregation. The pulpit cast its long shadow on the brilliant past and on my own dreams. My plans to save the children fell apart. I did not even know the fate of my own two children. I left our home in Ann's care. I had no key. I broke down the door and stepped into the uninhabited house.

"I Have a Bullet in My Back"

I, the mother, was alone with our two children and the young woman who lived in our home. Joel still did not return home, and in the morning I heard loud banging. Fearful of whom it could be, I rushed and cautiously opened the door just enough to peak and see. The cantor of the congregation, who lived on the same floor, stood there and turned to me and asked whether I heard the radio. Although the radio was turned on almost constantly in hopes that we hear a message from my husband, at that early hour in the morning, the radio was not on, and I learned only from him that the Russians returned and heavily bombed the capital city.

It seemed futile to hope for news from my husband. There would be no more messages through the radio waves. Worries. What will happen to us?

My sister called. Worried like me. She suggested that I get out of the house that is connected with the temple and congregational office and move into their apartment in the hospital where my brother-in-law worked as a neurologist.

I shared her concern about our safety. I packed a few necessities and moved with the children.

The turmoil gave birth to new opportunities. The police, most of the armed forces, and border guards looked upon the Russians as enemies and abandoned their posts. We learned that the borders were open. Long discussions followed. My brother-in-law suggested that we attempt to cross into Austria, and from there he would seek chances to immigrate to the United States where his uncles were well-known physicians.

I had to make difficult decisions. We did not hear from my husband. His fate and whereabouts remained unknown. The family urged me to go with them. I rationalized that it might be difficult to escape with small children, but if we all can find a way we could use that chance. If and when my husband would return, for him as a single person, would be easier to slip over the border. The rationalization worked. I hastily returned home. I did not look hard. I grabbed a small suitcase that I previously packed, not knowing what the days ahead would bring. I believed that some of the children's clothing and hygiene items were in the suitcase. I ran back to the hospital. Some members of my family were there, my mother, sister, husband and children, ready to move. My younger sister and family lived in a city closer to the border and she sent us a note that they already left. I got one step closer to making a decision.

My brother-in-law already organized our journey. A truck arrived, and we all climbed on the back where we could be covered and hopefully not seen.

Driving on the highway, Russians were everywhere. Shooting was heard all around. Our three-year-old daughter peaked from the truck and saw a Russian tank with its cannon turned in our direction. Suddenly as if having some deep pain, she yelled, "Mommy, I have a bullet in my back."

I attempted to console her, but to no avail, she was crying inconsolably. I again rationalized that it was just a childish fear and imagination. How little I knew that it left a deep scar on her soul and memory. Years later when we already lived in a large city in America that had a memorial park on the outskirts, we decided to go to the park. We packed the family in the car and we went. Arriving at the gate, our daughter burst out crying and screaming. She pointed at the a war memorabilia at the gate. An old canon was at the entrance. She shouted, "Mommy, I have a bullet in my back. Don't go in, don't go there."

Going back to the ride in the Hungarian truck, I remember that we moved for a while, and then the driver stopped. He came to the back and asked us to get off since the border was close, but with the truck he could not go any farther. We had to cross a shallow brook. On the other side there were Austrian Red Cross workers and they picked us up. We boarded their bus that took us to an armory in Vienna. The floor of the building was almost totally covered with mattresses, clean sheets, and blankets.

Tired and exhausted, I put the children to bed. They were sleeping, and I was dreaming that I was riding on the bus to visit my relatives for the holiday. I did not know that the visit would lead me to the wedding canopy. I was single and just like then, I was single again but under very different circumstances. My husband, the father of the children was not there. I dared to hope that he was safe.

I continued my dream. The children were safe. They would have the world of opportunities open ahead of them, whatever our future would be. I made the sacrifice for them and stepped into the unknown. I fell asleep.

The next morning, representatives of the welcoming countries came to visit and talked about possible destinations for us. I had no plans, but since I had a brother who already lived in France, I considered that option as one.

The American delegate invited us to take his bus and took us to the Embassy. There was a gentleman who spoke Hungarian. He saw my children and asked a few questions of me. I told him about my brother and France. He looked into my eyes, then at the children and with great sincerity said, "Get the hell out of Europe. Take them to America."

For our good fortune at the Embassy I met my mother, sister, husband and their daughter. They arrived sooner than we. The reunion was complete. It was much easier to arrive at a decision. It was a meaningful one.

While living on the crossroad of highways between Vienna and the center of Hungary, I watched with envy and secret longings the trucks and cars that delivered foreign aid. I stood at the window and I saw the American flag on the hoods of those vehicles. I dreamt that one day I would see more than the flags. I would be able to travel to America. I was only in Vienna, but I saw the American flag flying on the consulate building. My tears started running. My children would have a chance to succeed, to have a higher education that would have been denied of them in the country where they were born.I knew where I headed. The rest of my family put their application and the request for American sponsorship in motion already. They added the three of us. I needed to find out the address of the chief-rabbi of Austria. Before going to Vienna he was the rabbi of the congregation and lived in the same home I just left behind.

He welcomed us. His wife invited us to have a Sabbath dinner with them. He arranged hotel accommodations for us while waiting for our departure to the States. He offered his assistance while in the city. He was kind and helpful. Encouraged by his deeds, I asked him to keep a note for my husband in case he could escape. I knew that his first step would take him to see his colleague. I was ready to leave, but there was another great obstacle to overcome. All of us were taken to the airport for our flight. For some reason, unknown to me, the papers were in order for every member of the family, except the three of us. I frantically called the rabbi. He arranged our trip back to the hotel to spend the weekend there. Meanwhile, he did everything possible to correct our situation. He succeeded. In the middle of the following week we took off in a plane decorated with the flag of the United States. We had the most efficacious day to give thanks. We reached the land of the free on Thanksgiving Day. Then a new tradition began. Our religious holidays had an added one, Thanksgiving, celebrated with family every year.

THE NEW WORLD

Ann sometimes mentioned that young woman who was in my company when we first met. But the past was behind us. She did not represent any occasion to remember her. We knew that she married a man from my first congregation. We moved from my first congregation to my second pulpit that was quite a distance away. I devoted my life and energy to my congregation. Our lives followed new paths. The present seemed to be the time to live in.

But my life as a pulpit rabbi seemed to be suspended and interrupted for an unknown period of time when I left Hungary in 1956. I became a displaced person. I was bereft of clerical cloth. I had no books. I had only my title, rabbi, which I earned by being ordained. Still, the elongated shadow of the pulpit followed me. After having been in Vienna for a few weeks, I received a telephone call in my colleague's office. The caller asked me to officiate at the funeral of a five-month-old baby. He died of pneumonia, which he contracted while crossing the border at a cold snowy winter night. I hesitated to answer. I escaped with two shirts and one suit on my back. I was not even in the most presentable condition physically and mentally. Then came the word. It was the father, the member of my first congregation who married that young woman. In emotion–ridden words and sentences he asked me to officiate at the funeral. The past represented a commitment. I accepted the call. In the cemetery I saw the mother's painful tears. I identified with her sorrow. If Ann had not come to visit her cousin, maybe this baby could have been mine and hers. The mourners present, who shared the pain, were not aware of the pain I went through.

My life moved on. Since Ann refused to return to Vienna and continue from there to go to Israel, I applied for the visa to enter the United States.

The wheels of bureaucracy moved slowly. There were obstacles erected in every path. But the greatest issue was my conscience. In all my life, I decided that if ever I could leave the country of my birth and education, Israel was the only place I would go to settle.

Weeks passed. We exchanged several letters. In my letters I begged Ann to return to Vienna from where we would go to Israel, or go there directly and we should meet there. I did not understand what she wrote that she just left one war-torn country and she would not take the children to another one that was engaged in a war. I left Hungary at a time of great confusion and news block-out. Ann referred to the Sinai campaign of which I had no knowledge. I just repeated my suggestion to go to Israel. Ann had some additional experience in Vienna with officials that influenced her insistence to refuse my suggestions.

Ann had no information about me while I was still in Hungary under police surveillance and engaged in finding escape routes for hundreds of Jews. The scarcely available bits and pieces of information were contradictory. A childhood friend of mine in Israel turned to his governmental agencies and asked for some information about me. He received an official letter to the effect that while I attempted an escape, I was shot either by the border guards or the Russians patrolling the border area. It was not until Ann's sister and brother-in-law were contestants on the *$64,000 Question Show*, that she learned about my fate. Before they left for the show, Ann received a telegram from my colleague in Vienna that I escaped. My brother-in-law used their appearance on the show to make the announcement that I was alive and safe in Austria.

Ann insisted to remain in America with the children. The task for me was to work at removing the bureaucratic obstacles and reunite with the family as soon as possible.

Before that could happen we experienced something in an Austrian camp that was similar to whatever unveiled itself toward the end of 1956 uprising in Hungary. From Vienna we were taken on bus to Salzburg. It was late afternoon that the transport arrived. We were looking forward to be together, my brother, sister-in-law, their three year old, and my colleague, the chief rabbi of south-western Hungary with his family. It was not easy. The old guard, the Hungarian fascists were waiting for the bus with large kitchen knives in their hands. They were yelling that the Jews were in an advantageous situation again. They shouted that Jews had preferential treatment and were allowed to move into final relocation long before they could. The nights in the camp were not peaceful. Special guards were placed around our blocks where Jews were housed. I wrote a long report to the Hebrew Immigrant Aid Society representatives, but neither the letters nor the foreign official could change the minds of those who in their hatred were against us.

Finally Europe was behind us when the military transport ship arrived at Brooklyn Navy Yard on Valentines Day. Since it was a national holiday, our ship circled the area and we waited for the next day when the shipyard workers returned to their job. From early morning I was standing at the railing of the ship, looking and waiting. The clock moved at snail's pace. Then I spotted Ann. I was glad to see that she raised her hand a few times, smiled, and expressed in the waving of her hand how pleased she was that I was alive and soon reunited with the rest of my family after the months of separation. She wore a coat which I did not recognize. Later she told me that the Salvation Army received them on the Canary Islands and provided the sheer necessities for our children and the coat she wore.

It was still not time for the reunion. We were taken to Camp Kilmer in New Jersey. I had to stay there for processing; she returned to the family's new home in Coney Island.

Sunday she came to the camp and, as a person who already had a work permit and a job, became my sponsor and was given permission to take me with her.

My eyes were not wide enough to take in everything I saw. The large number of people everywhere, the labyrinth of the subway system at Times Square, the glitter of all the lights, the newness of the world just could not sink in.

The most memorable event of my life was just waiting for me. When we stepped in the crowded apartment, our three year old daughter in the arms of her mother, her thumb in her mouth, her wonderful smile on her lips, said in Hungarian, "Daddy, I knew that you would come."

Our new life began on holidays. Ann and the children landed in America on Thanksgiving Day. My ship reached Brooklyn Navy Yard on Valentine's Day. Although this holiday does not carry the same significance as Thanksgiving, it has become a memorable day in our lives, not for its old religious background but for the fact that after three months of separation and tumultuous events we reunited as a family.

The next morning, my wife, whom I thought could and should not work outside the home, went to her job in a necktie factory in Manhattan.

I stayed home. I had no job to go to. I had time to think. I was ordained. I had my rabbinic diploma, the Semikhah I committed my life to the pulpit. But of what worth was my diploma in a country where I did not feel at home I could not think of what I would do in a country where I did not understand the language. First I needed to find my place. In Hungary I knew where I belonged. I was a neolog rabbi. There was no neolog branch of Judaism in America. I knew ever since I was nine years old that I was not orthodox. I did not know the practices and principles of Reform. I had to decide. Although the neolog practice was closer to the American modern-orthodox, my decision was to choose Conservative Judaism. With considerable difficulty I was able to make an appointment with the Executive Vice-President of the Rabbinical Assembly.

This has become another memorable event. I was at the right place at the wrong time. Before my appearance he had a bad experience with another new arrival. It became known that the person lied about his credentials.

My wife and I met Rabbi Iceberg, although that was not his name. I presented my quest in Hebrew and asked for the favor to assist me in matriculating as a student in the Jewish Theological Seminary to learn the language. Among the series of unpleasant details, the most uncomfortable was that he derided my Hebrew and called a member of the teaching staff of Hungarian descent to translate my Hungarian to English. At the end of the interview, he said that he would not recommend me for matriculation in the school. Instead he advised me to go to some school, learn the language, apply for membership in the Rabbinical Assembly, and then get a congregation through its Placement Commission.

Before I mustered enough courage to make that telephone call and request an appointment, I went through an experience which became closely related to the feeling I experienced at the Rabbinical Assembly office. On the fourth day of my American life, my wife asked me to meet her in Manhattan after work. She gave me perfect written instructions how to take the subway and go the building whose number she jotted down on the paper. Armed with these instructions, I bravely traveled from Coney Island to Manhattan. I got off the train; walked up to the street and looked for the building. I was used to the Hungarian house numbering system. The houses were numbered in consecutive order on the odd and the even sides of the streets. I could not find that system on the buildings in New York. I became frightened. I got lost in the middle of the world's largest city. I had my piece of paper in my hand; I ran into stores to inqire, using my knowledge of German. Most of the people I approached did not understand what I was all about. I showed the paper in my hand. They could not recognize the house number. It was written in the manner we learned in our Hungarian schools. I had my Ph.D. in seven Semitic languages; I could correspond in Latin; I read Greek, and I spoke German. All that was of no help. My panic grew. Many thoughts swirled through my mind. I felt certain that I would not find Ann. She gave me directions to take the trains to Manhattan, but I had no idea how to return to our apartment. I ran up and down the street until I heard someone laughing behind me. It was Ann, my rescuer. She finished her work for the day and came down to the street. She spotted me. We returned home together. But my feeling remained. I felt panicky, humiliated, insecure, and hopeless. It began in the office at 123rd Street and Broadway. On the street my insecurity deepened. I found no relief. I felt lost.

I did not dare to think that, remaining true to my ardent hopes and desire, I could continue my life's calling. The Hebrew Immigrant Aid Society's clerk did not help either. At my first appointment, I had to fill out questionnaires. It seemed to be no problem. They were in Hungarian. I completed each form and on the bottom line I signed in the manner I usually did, writing the two letters Dr. as part of my signature. The officer, who happened to be the wife of a Seminary professor scolded me that I had no right to write Dr., only physicians could use that title in the United States.

At the end of the interview she inquired about my special skills. I mentioned that I studied graphic art, I could draw, and paint. She looked at a list in front of her, then turning to me she said that there was a job opening, stenciling numbers at freight cars. She gave me the address where I could apply for the job. In my humiliation, I became despondent. I could not hope to live even in the shadow of the pulpit. I did not apply for that position, but I had to support my family.

Subsequently I went to work in a fur factory as a floor boy, then as a packer-finisher in a garment factory; I cranked the copy machine in a Syrian yeshiva, and I went to study English. Six months later, I gained certification in New York and became a Hebrew School teacher in New England. The school was housed in a large synagogue. I used the opportunity to get back into the rabbinate. I assumed the responsibilities of an assistant rabbi. At the end of the two years, the synagogue officially created the position for an assistant rabbi. I called the senior rabbi, arranged an appointment to inform him that I wished to apply. His reply was another attack on my self-esteem. Although his wife was the daughter of a very prominent person who was born in a European country, he turned to me and said, "This job is not open for foreigners."

My dream did not change. I changed my reality. I continued studying. While immersing in my English studies, I discovered something that was frightening. I had a great ability to recall names, places, dates, quotes, page numbers. I prided myself that probably I could be awakened from my sleep and, when asked, I could go to my bookshelf, pick the relevant book and turn to the page and point my finger to the line where the answer was. I realized that most of my ability to recall was lost. I suffered a partial amnesia. I learned a new language and at the same time I was able to relearn most of what I lost. I conquered amnesia.

After many set backs, I became a member of the Rabbinical Assembly. The vice president was on a foreign mission. The professor who temporarily filled the position was very sympathetic to my plea. I asked for a congregation that had no Hungarians in a fifty-mile radius. It may sound like laughing matter. But I was serious.

Supporting my unusual request I told him that one Friday night while walking to services our children and I conspired. We were aware that Ann sought out Hungarians in all places where we lived. The articles of the conspiracy included our agreement that we shall not answer any questions directed to us in Hungarian; we either wouldn't reply or answer in English. When anyone of us would hear the phone at home, and Ann was available, we would not answer. She had to do it in English. Our conspiracy ended with good results. She learned English.

A small congregation in north-west New Hampshire, much smaller than 365 member families, elected me as their rabbi. We moved there by car. No approximate arrival time was established. It did not cool off the interest of the congregation. When we moved up to the driveway of the brand new home, the wife of the president stood there to greet us. Before we arrived, she filled up the refrigerator in the house with all kinds of necessities that we would suffer no need on the initial days of living there.

I wanted to continue my life as a pulpit rabbi. The pulpit waited for us and greeted us. We consider the three-and-a-half years we spent in that community extremely happy.

SHADOWS OF THE PAST

I was not aware that a dream can turn into a nightmare.

My dream became reality. I did not have to dream of the American flag with its stars and stripes. It was my country's flag. I lived and worked already in the United States. But at the awakening from the dream, the country was strange to me. I felt like a stranger in it. I did not speak the language. I could not read. When I watched television, I saw the action, but the sounds meant nothing. When I listened to the radio, the tunes were familiar, but the sounds that formed the words were flowing together, words I did not hear. My fear grew deeper and deeper.

My family forced me to answer the phone. They were not mean, they meant well. But I was terrorized. I answered the phone. In broken English I formed short sentences. As a reply, I heard the callers asking me to repeat what I said. The caller did not understand me; I could hardly recognize the words that came from the other end of line.

One new friend in good spirit once told me a joke about the greenhorn who walked into a restaurant. As soon as he was seated, the waiter handed him the menu, recited the specials, and the guest replied, "apple pie and coffee." The waiter thought that he heard only the last part of the order and asked, "will that be it?" The guest repeated, "apple pie and coffee." This was the only phrase the newcomer knew that could be used to order food in a restaurant.

The friend thought that the joke was funny. But it affected me in a different way. I felt dumb, ignorant. I was afraid that people would think that I was illiterate.

That feeling was terrorizing. Our children were in school. They had homework assignments. I was afraid that they would ask for my help. What would they think of me if I could not help them?

My past cast a shadow on me again. I remembered that at one time in my elementary school days, I went to a friend's house to do our homework together. As we went along, we ran into a problem. We were stuck. We could not proceed. I suggested to ask my friend's mother who was there, busying in the kitchen. She told me that her mother could not help us. I looked in the kitchen and said, "she is right there in the kitchen, let us just call her."

Panic-ridden she turned to me. "You must swear that you will never ever tell anybody. My mother can't help us, she does not know how to write or read."

I had never known anybody who was illiterate. I feared that my children might bring friends to do homework together, and if for some reason they would get stuck, they would turn to me for help. I feared that I would be unable to help, and they too would have to ask their friends never to tell anybody that I was illiterate. It was a recurring bad dream. A recurring nightmare. But it was not a night dream; it was a day time terror. I believe I could use a word one of our grandson's coined many years later when I almost took a wrong turn at the beginning of a divided highway on a foggy day. When I realized the mistake, I told him that it was like a nightmare. He corrected me, "No Gramma, it was a daymare."

I became increasingly aware that my tendency to seek out Hungarian speaking company was of no help to me. I began paying more attention to the radio programs. I listened to the lyrics. I began paying more attention to the words than the music. I used the words that I had learned to separate them from others in the songs. I repeated the words over and over again. I eagerly waited for the first chance to speak with someone and put the newly learned words into use. When it became clear that I used a new word correctly, and the listener understood what I said, the dark shadow, like the morning fog under the rays of the sun, began lifting. My days started becoming somewhat lighter.

The congregation, which called my husband to be its rabbi, was very nice to us. I was aware that one college graduate store owner, a board member visited my husband every Thursday morning in his office and went over his Friday night sermon paragraph by paragraph. He first corrected the mistakes in grammar then read each sentence into a tape recorder. Then Joel read the same text. In the afternoon he could listen to the audiotape over and over again, to practice the pronunciation by comparing the two versions.

Another member, a schoolteacher, recognized my difficulties, mostly from my withdrawn behavior, and offered her help. She came to our house twice a week with Dr. Seuss' books, and I learned *The Cat in the Hat*. It really takes only a small dose of thoughtfulness to build up one's confidence.

Children in their innocence can be more cruel with their honest statements than adults. I was very cautious with them in my fear that they would laugh at me. My fear turned frequently into delightful experiences when I listened to them and understood their logic that turns in the ears and eyes of the adults into humor.

I was delighted to hear a young boy to say when I introduced myself to him, "I know who you are. You are the Temple's wife."

Another boy was not less humorous when he asked me, "Does not the Rabbi have a license? When my mother drives me to Junior Congregation, I always see him walk."

The same youngster wondered whether the congregation provided him with housing. He asked, "Mom, doesn't the Rabbi have a home? He is always in the Temple."

I began to understand the serious talk of adults and the humor in little children's wisdom. I grew with them and their parents. They gave me room to grow, and I started feeling at home.

Life with that congregation meant three-and-a-half beautiful and meaningful years.

I also experienced fear and terror turn into delight. My husband is a perfectionist of the highest degree. That does not always make living with him easy. As we were accepted as a rabbi, his wife, and our children in our congregational roles and in the social life of our members, our comfort increased and we did not feel that we were refuges or foreigners.

But in New England one is always a newcomer.

My husband came home late one night, but he felt an urgency to tell me about an event at a board meeting.

One of the board members asked for the floor and in his usual manner stated his opinion quite forcefully. When he finished, the president turned to him, "How long have you been living here?" The man proudly replied, "Fifteen years." The president, as if he was poo-pooing the statement, motioned with his arm and hand and said, "So what? You are a newcomer."

After another meeting, with the full agreement of the school committee, my husband invited me, a newcomer, who struggled with the language for about three years, to teach the youngest children an hour every Sunday in the school.

It was a recognition, and as it turned out, a new door opener for me. It gave me the key to turn around, add a new dimension to my initial training, and find true joy and pleasure. It was a new accommodation within our marital relationship and a recognition of my desires. My husband, who initially was against my desire to work outside the house, invited me to take that job. I succeeded. My wish was heard. The old wise saying changed, "One can take the horse to the water and even teach him to drink."

A Change with Consequences

1962

In one's lifetime circumstances frequently require changes. Our children were growing, and we became concerned about what a small community's school system could offer as a good foundation and preparation for the future we dreamed of for them, and what they might have wanted for themselves. Our destiny took us to the Midwest. Soon we found out that the change carried consequences.

We arrived at our new destination by car the same way we moved to our previous post. The door to our new home was unlocked. It was a house that looked pleasant and seemed to offer comfort. The street was short, no heavy traffic, the aged trees provided shade and formed an arch-like canopy. We eagerly opened the door. No one waited to greet us. We were alone. So we joked that the trees provided the welcoming arch for us, like for the victorious general in ancient Rome who returned from battle or from war. Strangers, as we were, started wondering around the yard. A woman raised her hand from the adjacent home's yard in a welcoming move and came over to introduce herself. After exchanging the pleasantries she made a longer introduction and said that she and her husband were the owners of a seafood restaurant to which guests drove seventy or eighty miles for a dinner. She invited us for dinner at the restaurant. She even offered to take us there.

I was eager to introduce my family to the synagogue. We drove there before dinner. The office was still open; we could enter the building without any difficulty and in the foyer I proudly showed my family the fair-size brass plaque, which informed the visitor that the congregation was founded by the father of a well-known entertainer whom we all knew already from television.

After the short tour of the synagogue it was time to go for dinner. The atmosphere at the restaurant was comfortable, and we were looking forward to the beginning of the new phase of our lives.

The children began their schooling. I settled in the daily routine of the office, congregational duties, and school. Ann accepted the role which she assumed in the previous congregation and hoped to enjoy teaching in the regular schedule of the larger school.

Dreams do not always turn into realities. Our son frequently came home from school crying. He was a sociable child, but his classmates were not greeting him with open arms. He wanted to participate in school and after-school activities, but the others were more than reluctant to accept him. Our daughter, three years younger, could not put her feelings into words as clearly as her brother, but her pain was similar.

I accepted the position in that city with the understanding that the congregation was affiliated with the Conservative movement. I came from a European country where the division of the Jewish population was different than in the U.S. I gave serious consideration to the decision to become an American Conservative rabbi. I studied the standards for Conservative synagogue life, the history of the Conservative movement, the ideas of its leading thinkers, and the deliberations of its Committee on Jewish Law and Standards. I thought I was well prepared to follow and, if necessary, implement that knowledge. There was room for implementation. The congregation fell within the principle and decision I made about size I wanted to serve. I went about visiting the members. I learned about the demography of my new congregation. I found the families' composition quite different than expected. Due to the circumstances the leaders and members of the congregation lived within much more relaxed boundaries than the written standard for Conservative congregations suggested. In my idealism, I hoped I could lead the flock toward a more observant life style. As it turned out my ideas and those of the congregants were not even close to each other. My moves and suggestions found much more resistance than I envisioned. Every change, even a most basic one, met non-acceptance if not outright rejection. My suggestions created disharmony.

My attempt to reorganize, rather organize, the school seemed to find favor with the school committee. The committee liked that Ann accepted the teaching assignment without requiring any remuneration. They talked of Ann's work in the school with appreciation.

The appreciation of this kind taught her a lesson. When it came to another time and another change in our lives, she accompanied me to one of the interviews. In the course of the conversation a member of the search committee turned to her and asked what she would do for the congregation, if I was elected. With all seriousness, without any of her usual hesitation she turned to the questioner and addressing the whole group, said, "Gentlemen, if you are electing my husband as your rabbi, I, his wife, will move here with him." (Is that a small step out of the shadow?).

With all seriousness, I believe her answer did not come out of the blue sky. A few weeks prior to that interview the well-known entertainer, the son of the congregation's founder, was invited by the sisterhood to provide an evening of good times. He was our house guest. The president of the sisterhood came to welcome the guest. The conversation was cordial, and the president finally came out with a topic of importance. She gave a short briefing of the sisterhood's non-profit status and the poor financial state of the organization. She asked for the guest's consideration that the honorarium be different than at other places and asked him to accept a smaller amount.

The answer came swiftly and sternly, "Madame, my honorarium is such and such. It is not negotiable."

The president reached into her pocket book and wrote a check for the designated amount. The performer accepted it with an appropriate thank you, then placed it in his wallet.

This move was followed by another one. The entertainer took his check book and his pen and began writing. When completed he tore the check and handed it to the president. The amount was identical with the requested honorarium. An explanation followed. "Madame, my honorarium is set according to the value of my performance. It is due to me. What I do with the money I earn is my business. Turn this amount to the best way the sisterhood can use it."

Our children's relationship with the son of our next-door neighbor did not turn out as pleasant as the incident of the entertainer with the sisterhood president. To our delight they had no experience of any discrimination or prejudicial treatment because of our religion. But one day our son approached us with a question, "What does Heil Hitler mean?"

We were shocked and instead of answering him, we asked where he heard the expression. He went on to say that the son of our next door neighbor told him that he liked to watch German war movies and he knew that those words meant that the Jews were bad people. Our son asked us, "Are we bad people and why are we bad?" Our son sadly learned that he was excluded not only at school, he was on the street just as well. He could not associate any longer with the boy of whom he thought was his friend.

Our move to the larger community had its consequences. The sunny days of three-and-a-half years in the previous congregation slowly became memories, and the sun of our newly-dawned days lost their brightness and the shadows grew longer. Our conversations at the end of the days centered around the conditions of our lives.

Ann saw that my situation was getting more difficult. She wanted me to succeed, to increase the opportunities that could provide spiritual experiences, a clearer understanding of being affiliated with the Conservative movement, and gain even if a minimal appreciation for our efforts. She knew from the comments and compliments she heard that her work met the approval of the constituents. She did not want to steal the lime light. She held back herself. She began working in the background. She was moving deeper in the shadow of the pulpit.

She knew that I was a warm and caring person, and was able to establish warmer contacts in the living rooms of people, than on the pulpit and at board meetings. My conversations were friendly, provided information, presented religious issues from a point well considered. There was a clearer understanding of my thinking and the expectations of the members were met easier when I was sitting with them on the same level, than when I was speaking down from the heights of the pulpit. In the hopes that people would know another side of me, Ann introduced customs that the congregation had not experienced before. In the two years we spent there, she arranged open houses on Rosh Hashanah afternoon, Simhat Torah morning after services, and provided fun and entertainment at our Hanukkah parties. The result was interesting. During one of our vacations when we were out of town, the board called an emergency meeting. Based on unsubstantiated grounds regarding the school administration, a decision was made that my contract would not be renewed. The decision was conveyed to me in a manner that was considered humorous, "We would love to retain her. She can stay, but your contract will not be renewed."

The seeds of our efforts did not fall on fertile soil. Being still new in the country, this decision, whether I wanted to admit or not, affected my self esteem. Although we hoped to overcome the sadness of the experience, for years we frequently talked about it. In our conversations we avoided using the name of the community, we referred to it as "blank." Ann felt hurt for me. She believed that she knew me on a much deeper level than the people of the congregation. She saw my efforts, endured the consequences of my actions, the long lonely hours of the day, and the silence in the house without me being present at night. She still considered our work a shared task for the sake of people and hoped for some satisfaction for us.

At that time some of our dreams parted ways. Unconsciously I continued living the dream which my family had for me. I made a conscious effort to provide a model, an example for our children. My secret desire was that our son would attend the Seminary to become a rabbi, and probably become a better rabbi than his father. I continued cherishing the years of my youth I spent in my rabbi's office and home. My waking hours led me to thoughts about a dream of a future that had not been realized.

"What would have happened if there was no World War II, no Holocaust?" My attachment to those memories grew stronger with the passing of days. The periodic disappointments I experienced in the congregational rabbinate did not destroy my dream. But his mother, some times half seriously at others half jokingly, used to say, "My lullaby and bed time story (which she never missed) will tell our son that he must not become a rabbi."

We did not exactly know whether it was a good job for a nice Jewish boy, and in those years we could not even think that it was good for nice Jewish girls to take on the challenge.

A LONG RIDE AND A LONGER STAY

1964

It was the time for another move. The experiences behind us were mixed. Some were pleasant, some eye-openers. The Midwest was not the same that we got accustomed to in New England. The New England life style said something like this: "Even if I make $80,000 dollars a year, I remain frugal and spend as if I made only $10,000." I consistently taught tolerance and preached against generalization. I still judged the mid-western life-style that people enjoyed the remodeled carriage houses, the larger cars and the circular driveways, in a general sense that it expressed a desire to show that one made $80,000, although the actual income was $10,000.

I was looking for an atmosphere that was closer to my ideas and ideals. I hoped to find that in our new location, back in New England. The ride in the car was long, we covered many miles. When we reached the outskirts of the city of our new home, old memories started emerging. As a ninth-grader, I was not doing my best in geography. On two occasions I missed to answer the questions. Once I was asked about the Hungarian town that was known worldwide for its chicken farms and egg production. The other question was where in the world was the largest, one-mile-long, industrial building. I saw the building that I have not seen before, yet it left a mark on my self esteem. It was on the other side of the river from the highway.

The memory that I could not answer the question where the world's longest industrial building was painful. My fate was repeated. I had been the rabbi of the Hungarian community that was known for its chicken farms. In the U.S.A. I became the rabbi of the community where the world's largest industrial building complex was located.

I was glad I was not superstitious. I did not allow myself to think that this experience was foreshadowing future events. But we had some surprises.

My first new experience was that the congregation did not provide housing for the rabbi and his family. My predecessor owned a home and offered to rent it to us since it stood unoccupied from the time he moved to his new congregation. We accepted his offer. But I wanted to own a property rather than renting a house. My parents had a small lot in Hungary. But with the anti-Jewish legislation in the 1930s, the government confiscated the land. Under the subsequent communist rule no private property could be had. We came to the land of the free. The opportunity presented itself to become landowners in an American city. But there were conditions to meet. The house had to be built within walking distance from the Temple that was built in a densely populated residential area. Days of searching led to no find. One day while approaching my office in the Temple, I passed by a nice wooded area. Just a narrow alley separated this lot from the synagogue building. It seemed large enough to meet the city's zoning requirements. I talked to the two families who lived on the two sides of the lot. They did not own the land and did not know who its owner was. Fortunately a few members of the congregation were lawyers. One of them, an old-timer, researched the deed, found the owner, and began negotiations about the purchase.

I designed a house, not knowing that after a few years of study, our son would become an architect. He designs larger and more efficient edifices than I did. We hired a builder, and the construction began. It took a year, and we moved into our new home.

Owning a house for me became a bittersweet experience. I thought that since the rabbi and his family occupied the house, it was a "parish house." I presented my idea to the Board of Directors and asked that the congregation designate it the home of their rabbi and ask for the tax-free recognition. One board member made the motion not to accept the proposal, reasoning that all home owner members paid their taxes, the rabbi should not be an exception. I gladly paid our taxes and thus contributed to the welfare of the community, which accepted us and provided the education necessary for our children.

The close vicinity of our house to the synagogue and my office provided means to maintain family ties. Although I worked long hours seven days a week, I was not totally separated. My wife through the kitchen window, and I through the window of my office could see each other and send our secret signals to each other during the day. She liked the new way of communication, it forced me to keep my word. If it seemed that I forgot my promise and commitment to be home for dinner with Ann and the children, she just raised her hand, waved the threatening signal, and I knew that it was time to get off my chair, leave the desk, and walk the few steps that separated us only physically during the day.

Advantage is usually connected with disadvantage. My beloved rabbi in one of his humorous moments told us that he had the most devoted congregation in the country. The men were seated in the main sanctuary and the women took their seats on the balcony that was built on the three sides of the building. He talked about his very devoted, spiritually inclined congregation where all men raised their eyes toward heaven and the women bowed their heads toward to the main floor in true humility in faithful prayer. It seemed that this memory of my young adulthood repeated itself. Saturday mornings, the members of my congregation turned to the life-giving sunshine. Their eyes were protected, they did not look directly into the blinding rays of the sun, they watched the rabbi's wife who was suntanning in the backyard while waiting for the rabbi to return home for the Sabbath meal, and have lunch with the whole family. She preferred the direct sunshine outdoors to sitting in the Temple in the shadow of the pulpit.

It is interesting how circumstances can turn the most pleasant thoughts into double-edged swords. Owning our home provided us with stability. I was proud and happy with this new turn in our lives and made it known to the membership and the leadership of the congregation that my family and I considered making the city our permanent home. This statement had an effect on my future contract negotiations and salary arrangements.

I slowly integrated myself in the life of the general community. I was invited to sit on boards and committees, I was elected to offices and some organizations elected me as their president. In one of these capacities I became involved with the planning board of a new private high school. It turned out that it was started mostly as an interest of the Jewish population. Maybe it was for public relations, maybe a genuine recognition of our position in the community, the new school's board offered tuition free education to our daughter. The offer was attractive and inviting. Our decision came after a long series of conversations. I gratefully declined to accept it since I firmly believed in good public education.

Our children settled in their public schools and we directed our attention to the synagogue's and its school's programs. Ann apparently forgot the statement she made at the interview she attended with me in another congregation. I had one contract, the one-salary one-contract theory did not materialize. She gave in to my suggestions and started teaching without compensation. Then when our children grew in age and in knowledge, I convinced them to lead our Junior Congregation services since it was scheduled at the time of the adult services on Saturday mornings. They did it with enthusiasm, and our young children responded to them. But when they received letters of acknowledgment, I had to keep it a secret that the letters were dictated or written by their father and not the chair of the education committee or the board.

WAR AND PEACE—REWARD AND PUNISHMENT

Our new post did not require any change in the principles and old decisions Joel made. The membership was under 365, and we soon began visiting the families who belonged to the synagogue. Since there were children in the process of preparation for their Bar and Bat Mitzvah celebrations, these families were our priorities. Many years later it has been proven that the first two of these families became our close friends. It was an unusual experience. Our previous experience was that families with whom we could maintain closer ties, lived in the congregations which we left. Although not through conscious research, we found out that the rabbi's wife and the rabbi live under specific conditions that it is not advantageous to open up with the details of our private lives to members of the congregation in the community where we lived. Maybe we still held some of our suspicion from the times we lived under the searching eyes of built-in spies and were cautious that intimate pieces of information could be used against us even by people whom we thought could be trusted.

Although once I expressed my opinion that the rabbi's contract meant one job for one person, I agreed to teach without compensation because we agreed that our goal was to build a well-organized school from the fragmented unorganized small groups of students who had instruction when their teacher, the previous rabbi, was not called to deal with other pressing activities.

The building did not have a sufficient number of classrooms. We needed to use any available space for the afternoon and evening classes. We faced unsurmountable difficulties. The congregation pleaded that it had no reserves and operated on an almost poverty level. Something happened, which, with hindsight, appears hard to believe. The rabbi was not given an office of his own. The Board insisted that he had to share an office with "his" secretary. In reality, the person was the secretary of the congregation with debatable loyalties to the rabbi.

Accepting the poverty plea, we put our energies into directing the congregational activities on a forward path.

By the time of the High Holidays, we got acquainted with the families of school age children, the shut-ins, and the elderly.

I was surprised when on the first day of Rosh Hashanah my husband suggested that instead of going home from services to have lunch, we go together to visit two sick elderly members to provide them with hearing the shofar sounds that they missed due to their inability to attend the synagogue services. The walk was quite long. The welcome by the first family was rewarding. After exchanging a few niceties, we were told that they were really not strictly observant, but appreciated our effort to give them the opportunity to hear the shofar.

The second home presented a different experience. When he was well, the man of the house was a regular attendant at services. He was known as the man who offered his prayers in such a loud manner that the cantor could have been proud and happy to have a voice like his.

Joel explained the purpose of our visit, and the elderly couple seemed to be grateful. When he blew the shofar the same identical way as he did at the synagogue service, the gentlemen informed him that he did not do it right and engaged in a long instruction telling him how he should have done it. We waited for the end of the lecture, looked at each other, and left with a heavy heart.

For the ensuing years the High Holidays were the highlights of the rabbi's activities. One year, Joel asked me to give him a few minutes of my time. Not knowing what his intentions were, I sat close to him and listened to his difficulty with the compliments he heard at the reception line following the services. One member, probably wanted to be complimentary, told him while shaking his hand, "Rabbi, your sermon was magnificent. How can you top this next year?"

I had my share on the pulpit. We agreed that our goal was to have as many members of the congregation, as many were willing, participate in the services. It was the time when women awakened and wanted to have more participation in the synagogue service than they had in the years of male domination. I firmly believed that the Haftarah, the prophetic portion of the service, on the first day of Rosh Hashanah, which deals with the fervent desire of a mother to have a child, should be chanted by a mother or certainly by a woman. After all voices were heard at the gatherings of the Ritual Committee, it was agreed that I would be given the honor. When I ascended the rostrum, to many people present it was shocking, but it was proven that women, too, can do what men do (better?).

I gained my right to be on the pulpit. During the summer every year Joel prepared enhancements, meditations, introductions to eminent parts of the service. After having the necessary number of volunteers, he discussed and rehearsed these parts with those members who accepted to present them. One year he asked me to talk before the Martyrology portion of the Memorial prayers as a survivor of the European Holocaust. While speaking, memories flooded within me. My tears started rolling down my cheeks, and I had to stop for a short while to regain my posture. When I returned to my seat, a male member approached me and said, "Do you know why I came to services? I came because it is a holiday, not to watch you cry."

There was no permanent cantor to conduct services during the year, but for the High Holidays some change was accepted. Instead of using the different caliber talents of the individual members to lead the prayers, it was decided to hire a cantor for those four days of the year. I was eager to be of any help I could. Before the cantor came, I invited him and his family to have their meals with us. After the first day of the services, I waited for them that I could walk the short distance to our house with them. The wait was quite long. I had no idea what happened. We found out that one influential old-timer stopped the cantor and invited him and the family to his home. The cantor said that they already received the invitation from the rabbi. The man expressed his disapproval, "You know, Rabbis come and go, but remember, members stay!"

Passover is my favorite holiday, and the High Holidays are second. I enjoy the preparation, the intimate atmosphere, the family around the table, and love to watch the faces while they read the Rosh Hashanah sentiments, expressed in the letters which I place under everyone's dinner plate.

The impact of the adherence to religious and family traditions has a long shelf life. I cannot be sure whether our observance was a cloud that locked out the sunshine casting a shadow, or it was the shadow of the pulpit that grew so long that it dimmed the brightness of our joy.

The many joys, achievements, and successes we derived from living with our congregations were just as much part of our lives as the lives of our children. But at the same time it formed and shaped our children's ideas about relationships, and religious principles. We knew what the model was we consciously provided. With perfect hindsight I can see what Joel wanted to accomplish without ever verbalizing his ideas. He was strict. He believed that his family should live in accord with his beliefs and project an image identical with his toward the congregation. Our children reacted to that effort according to their personality.

Our son, who missed attending his school's extra curricular activities when they coincided with our holiday observances, developed a way to reframe his experiences. For him, as he stated as an adult, it was an education to turn every deprivation into a virtue. If he could not go to a school dance, he looked at it as an opportunity to spend time with his family, or turned the hours, spent at home and not with his friends, into active study periods.

Our daughter is cut out of a different material. She did not like to be different than any of her friends. On Fridays she wished to be Christian (especially after the consumption of meat was allowed), on Saturdays she wanted to belong to the Muslim community (that observed Friday as the Sabbath), and on Sunday she was content to be Jewish. One Saturday afternoon she approached her father and announced that she was bored and wanted to draw pictures. Dad said that she could not draw since it was not a Sabbath activity and suggested another way to overcome boredom. She could play an important role if she set up some chairs in her room, and teach a class, pretending that the chairs were her students. With the most honest sincerity she turned to her father, "Dad, let's pretend that today is not Sabbath, and I can draw."

In our experience the rabbi's children have a good mixture of pleasant and unpleasant experiences. There is no umbrella that could protect them from the vicissitudes of public life. We were out one night visiting some friends. When we returned, we found our daughter in tears, very frightened. She could hardly gather enough courage to tell us what affected her. While we were away, a man–who was a member of the other congregation in town–phoned the house and, since we were not home, left a message with her. It was the end of October, around the anniversary of the Hungarian uprising against the Russian oppression in 1956. One of the local radio stations invited her father to be on a talk show to discuss the events of that time in Hungary. The man's message was that her father should be very careful, if he would appear on radio talk shows, he would be chased out of town. She cried inconsolably and just repeated the question, "Daddy, are you going to lose your job, and we will have to move again?" Her father's reassuring words, that we don't have to be afraid of the threats of a man who carried some kind of a grudge against the radio station, did not calm her down. The insecurity, the fear of being uprooted, and possibly be exposed to non-acceptance as in the previous city's school, left a mark on her tender soul.

I felt a need to keep away from this kind of experience and for a few weeks a year just to be me. We followed Joel's decision to give our children a model of an observant American Conservative Jewish family. We were just rebuilding our lives. We needed to learn more to know exactly that our life style was giving them that model. Our income could not cover the tuition and enrolment fees for two children in Camp Ramah where they could experience first hand Conservative Jewish living. A truly good friend of my husband, a rabbi of a large congregation in another state, suggested that I go to work in Camp Ramah, and that my salary would cover the children's camp expenses at least partially. My training in Hungary came handy. I applied and was hired as a camp nurse. For ten consecutive years I worked at the American and Canadian camps of our movement. The children learned the spirit of conservative Judaism. I believe that these and other experiences led them to accept that on their sixteenth birthday they did not get a car or the car key from their parents, but a round trip ticket to Israel. The arrangement was that they spent eleven weeks in the homes of their father's childhood friends. Our son returned with a functionally good Hebrew. Our daughter, with her compassionate spirit, spent a good deal of time with the mothers of our friends who did not speak Hebrew. She followed her independent mind, she came home not with the knowledge of Hebrew language, as we hoped, but with a good Hungarian.

While I was the nurse in the camp, my husband visited me as frequently as he could. He became known to the camp director and the staff, and after a few years, he was invited to teach a few courses in the camp. I let him speak of these experiences in his own words.

TEACH AND LEARN

Thirty years in the congregational rabbinate taught me that if I want to achieve something I needed the courage to speak up.

When I decided to leave the country of my birth, I left behind my security that I felt in my profession and my position.

The move, the new ways of life, unfamiliarity with my position, role, duties, and opportunities had an effect on my feeling of security.

After having moved from one continent to another and changing positions three times, I desired to make our lives as permanent as possible. I was a greenhorn and insecure, unfamiliar with the conditions. When I was introduced to the existing facility of my new congregation, and I saw that the building did not even have enough classrooms to facilitate the smooth operation of the school, although shocked, trusting decency and loyalty I accepted accepted an arrangement as inevitable. I convinced myself that the congregation went as far financially as they could. I raised no objection that I would have an office shared with the Temple's secretary who could do the secretarial work for me.

When it came to the time that I had to counsel and hear confidential personal issues, I realized what a mistake it was to agree so easily and not to raise my objections that an office shared with the secretary would hinder the delivery of my services. In my mind the best I could do was to see people with personal issues in their home, or after office hours. I believed that since the secretary was paid for the time spent on the job, I could not ask her to leave the office to assure the confidentiality which the nature of my work required.

A painful experience taught me to demand the minimally necessary conditions that would allow me to fulfil my duties as rabbi. It came to my attention that the secretary overheard a confidential issue that a young man presented to me. I was not aware of the close relationship the secretary had with the family, especially with the father of the young man. The father was a long time board member. When he learned that I promised confidentiality to his son, he viewed my promise as a conspiracy against him.

When I found out the betrayal, I found out that there was a solution. I demanded a separate office. The room adjacent to the office was used as a regular classroom. The secretarial office was moved there.

I had my office, but my privacy was still not assured. Going to the secretary's office next door, attending services in the chapel, or setting up the social hall, people passed my office that had a plain-glass window. Instead of requesting a door without a window, my ingenuity suggested to cover the glass with a sheet of paper that displayed a religiously inclined cartoon. At a board meeting a serious answer was demanded to the question, what the rabbi was doing in his office that he had to hide behind a window covering.

This and similar questions prepared the ground for the long-time board member and his group of organized friends to begin a campaign against the renewal of my contract. They planted the seeds of doubt that if the rabbi had to hide things from the congregation, he probably had to hide other information, too. They spread the rumor that the rabbi pretended to have a Ph.D. (The original diploma on the wall of the office was not convincing when vicious rumors wanted to reach a predetermined goal.) Although they did not get enough votes at their first trial, the foundation of my trust was shaken.

The words of our daily morning prayers, to learn and to teach, became an important point to ponder. As Ann mentioned, our financial state was not sufficient to cover the registration of two children at Camp Ramah every summer. She relied on her first professional training and for ten years spent the summers as a nurse in several of our movement's camps. Through my presence as a visitor I became known among the members of the Rabbinical Assembly and the Ramah offices, I was invited to teach subjects that fell within my range of knowledge and interest. First I accepted a job as a teacher for one four-week period of my summer vacation. One year my teaching assignment would have required my presence for the whole summer. I approached the chairman of the congregation's Personnel Committee and he consented to my request to present it to the full board. At the end of four weeks, a friend called me in camp and suggested that it would be in my interest if I immediately returned home because "something was brewing."

At home I learned that the Board, especially the president demanded my return since I left without the permission of the Temple leadership. I was not aware that the chairman, who agreed to my taking the camp position, never consulted the president, the Board as a whole or its individual members.

The behavior of the same president was quite different at another incident. He sympathized with the group who sought a change and worked for not renewing my contract. It was the time of his son's Bar Mitzvah celebration. In his usual manner he did not inform me in direct communication. He hired a messenger, another long time board member to approach me and ask for a favor on behalf of the president. The favor was to allow him to invite the previous rabbi who was very friendly with the family to officiate at the service when his son was going to celebrate his becoming a Bar Mitzvah. Being a greenhorn and a person with a damaged sense of security, I did not live by my right. I did not insist that it was my pulpit, and it was my privilege to provide services to the membership. I did not even mention that the proper protocol required that the rabbi call me and ask my permission to be part of the service as an invited friend. The messenger suggested that it would be helpful if I took my vacation at that time. He suggested that it would give us a chance to fulfill our desire to take a trip to Israel around that date. Blindly and deafly I did not see any harm in the suggestion. I worked with the Bar Mitzvah candidate for four years in the congregation's school, spent a year on his special preparation, and all was in order.

Upon return home from vacation we learned that I was accused of delinquency and neglect of my duties. I took my vacation and left the president's son unprepared for his Bar Mitzvah service. the family had to hire a private tutor to complete the instruction and invite a rabbi from another community to conduct the service.

A different set of circumstances in which I was involved with Camp Ramah provided other learning experiences. It was our daughter's six-teenth (sweet sixteen) birthday, and I planned to spend that day with her in camp. In the morning I left town with the knowledge of the board. I was driving on the turnpike when suddenly I saw the state police cars fol-lowing me with the flashing lights on. I pulled over. The officer informed me that he knew who I was from the special number plate on my car. He had an order to demand my immediate return because there was a death in the congregation and the family wanted immediate consultation regarding the funeral arrangement.

Live and learn is a phrase, but in one case learning was not about life it was about death. We received the sad news that my father died in Hungary where he remained after his sons and their families left. My grief and sorrow deepened when I learned that I could not attend his funeral and observe the days of morning with his widow. I planned the traditional week-long seclusion in privacy here with my family. Within the seven days of my morning two deaths occurred in the congregation. Neither the cemetery committee, nor the ritual committee, nor the Board as a whole, looked for a rabbi who could officiate at those funerals. It was silently expected that I would interrupt my week of mourning to live up to my contractual responsibilities.

I learned it from my father, it was taught in my schools, that a rabbi is a public servant, and his professional duties override his personal life. I turned the lessons I learned into practice. Thirty years on the pulpit pro-vided me with valuable experiences which probably I could not have gotten in any other profession. I can state without hesitation that I enjoyed every hour and every minute meeting the needs of congregations. In our work certain rewards are not immediate. It is a hidden reward to receive a note from an adult that a word, a statement, an idea heard in childhood in the afternoon school left a meaningful mark on the person's life. It is not an immediate reward, like a compliment that some of our students, male and female, decided to continue their education and became rabbis. I trust I can say without arrogance that their decision meant that I provided a model which they judged worthy of realizing in their lives. There are delayed rewards in the tears of joy when unexpectedly from thousands of miles away someone sends a poem reflecting on one or more experiences that involved me and my family. It makes life worth living. It is worth the energy that repays much later. It means that I dropped something along the journey, someone picked it up and uses it to enrich that someone's life. In order to grow (rather than expand) on the pulpit I needed observing eyes and open ears to pick up these signals at the time when it came to 'rechannel my energies' which is another way for me to retire.

WHOSE LINE IS IT ANYWAY?

Times change, and we change within them. I am a happy woman to live in an era of history when–I believe–changes come much faster than ever before. But since God's mills work slowly, change does not come easy. It is easier to reject change than accepting it.

I was touched by the winds of the times. I live in a time when 'egalitarian' became a household word in more liberal circles of the secular and religious world. Slowly it is becoming accepted that not only our forefathers' virtues are exalted in our prayers. The contributions of their wives, the mothers of our people, began receiving their deserved recognition.

There was a time, in the sixties and seventies, when experimentation was welcome in synagogues. So called innovative services were offered. Family services with changed time-tables and mixed seating became the norm in most non-orthodox synagogues. The long black robes were left in robing rooms. Rabbis and cantors appeared more human. They did not sound like speaking thundering words from the heights of their pulpits. Officiants and congregation -at least physically- became closer.

I talked frequently with my family about words, statements, and thoughts in our prayer books that sounded foreign to me and did not reflect either my philosophy or theology. I found it difficult to offer words in prayers which I could not believe, or utter thousands of years old philosophical statements which developing science contradicted and eliminated. In these discussions I referred to my experiences, broadcasts, and television interviews from space with astronauts and pictures of our earth they transmitted. When I read the words of the psalm with the congregation in our prayer book that "God established the earth upon flowing waters," my mind flashed pictures of thinkers burning at the stake because they dared to think, write, and say that the earth was not flat. Some of these words and thoughts expressed in our prayers did not inspire me, did not add spiritual fervor to my devotion–*kavanah* as our people say in Hebrew-, rather they engaged me in philosophical thought and scientific discoveries, while I was praying.

My mother tongue is not English. I did not master Shakespearian English. I found it strange to address God in prayers as Thou, Thee and Thine, in words that are not part of my daily conversation, not that of my contemporaries' either, and talk about God at home with our children and my students in the classroom as He, Him, His, You and Yours. I yearned to speak to God the same manner I speak to those whom I love.

My exchanges with Joel convinced me that our thoughts were similar. Long before I verbalized or put my thoughts into writing here, I recognized that congregations were willing to recite responsively or in unison whatever was printed in the books. Even those who were considered rebels by the congregation rarely raised these or similar issues with the rabbi in their homes or in the privacy of his office. He also believed that other than patina-covered words were also sacred for prayers. He accepted poems of contemporary writers, thoughts of thinkers of our times, the lyrics and tunes of new musicians who spoke clearly to the young and the mature equally inspiring. He put his beliefs into practice. I watched how much time, thinking, and consideration he put into creating services that could breathe fresh spirit into the prayers of adults, young adults, and children. He had another issue with the way services were contacted. In our time, it is difficult to keep people and their attention for three-hour-long services. He disliked the manner in which services were shortened. He did not want to instill in people that we offered incomplete services by turning to page 42 after page 16 just for the sake of shortening the length. He composed services and printed them that they were complete, followed from cover to cover. I agreed with him that the new prayer books were unsatisfactory. Some of them invented artificially sounding words and long phrases to avoid mentioning that our ancestors believed in a God who was male. So God was not male anymore, but was not changed into female either. The new editions of prayer books-supposedly gender sensitive-deepened my dissatisfaction. Here and there the mothers of our people were mentioned along with the fathers. In the translation the wording made serious strides to convey female equality, but it did not come across from the traditional Hebrew text. The body of the text remained unchanged. God was still male and we addressed Him with all the attributes and action words as male. I labeled it "intellectual dishonesty." I acknowledged that it is difficult to become gender sensitive without restructuring the entire edifice of the time-honored Hebrew prayers. But as it is now, it is inconsistent, and only a half-hearted effort is made to bring the entire prayer book in line with our contemporary realities.

I did not know at that time that my husband also struggled with these issues and changed some words, phrases, and sentences in his personal prayer book which he used at the services. One day, I had something to do in the Temple. I was there close to the end of the morning service. Some of the men were still lingering engaged in conversation. I was in the adjacent room, the door was open. When I recognized that the topic of the conversation was the rabbi, I started paying attention. One man loudly questioned the rabbi's authority to change words in the prayer book. When asked by the other men for more information, to support his statement, he went on to tell the story. When the rabbi left, he looked in the drawer of his prayer stand and found that in his prayer book on almost every page words were altered.

I was not spying. I did not want to overhear other people's conversation. But I felt justified and excused. I gained a very important insight into how my husband was viewed. He was sincere, he gave serious consideration to expressing his strong belief when making those changes. Hearing this conversation, I felt like I was on a battlefield and I was wounded. Joel's best intentions were turned against him, the person. He wanted to bring the form and the spirit of prayers closer to the contemporary style and living conditions and he was viewed as a person who destroyed ancient sacred cows. Even more, it was turned into a personal issue questioning his authority as the rabbi, the local interpreter of Jewish law and custom and the judge of words. It was questioned whose words were sacred and whose more sacred.

A little knowledge is dangerous. I wished the men, who discussed the rabbi's violation of sacred words, had seen the words of a sage, Samuel David Luzzatto, who wrote in the prayer book he composed, "Our forebears established for us the norm for prayers how to praise God and how to pray before God. They did not, however, intend with their regulation to make the form of prayer fixed and unchangeable, to make it impossible to add or subtract....Our Sages did not put in writing our prayers and blessings in book form. They permitted every individual to lengthen or shorten (the prayer) in accordance with his or her wisdom. That is why Rabbi Eliezer said, 'He who recites his a prayer in a routine manner, his prayer cannot be a supplication for God's grace.'" (Mahzor B'nai Roma)

The incident happened quite a few years ago. My wound is still there. But some kind of medicated ointment was spread over it. When the publication committee of our movement worked on a new daily prayer book, the editor sent unpublished drafts to a few of the general membership. Joel was involved for years already in thinking about writing a book that would have dealt with the origin of one Hebrew name of God. As a reply to the draft, he submitted his observation about that issue. There was never an acknowledgment of his thoughts or contribution, but his suggested change was included in the new prayer book. Later we observed that the usual rendition of God's name in translations was changed not only in that prayer book, other segments of American Jewry included the untranslatable personal name of God, Adonai, in their prayer books.

No one besides the members of the publication committees might know how the change came about. We know.

The unsolicited information from different sources, remarks made in face to face conversations, personal written and spoken communications with colleagues and their families moved me to see that America and

Hungary are not only different continents, also the conditions under which we live are different. My husband and all other rabbis in Hungary were qualified and authorized by their ordination to preach, teach, and be part of the religious judiciary. By virtue of their election to a congregation they were granted life-time tenure. This gave them the authority to express their judgment on all issues freely. Their opinion was requested, sought, and accepted in a wide range of issues from financial planning to religious law and observance.

In America, I recognized how difficult the rabbi's, probably every rabbi's position is. The world around him is divided into two camps. Uncertainty looms every time when contracts are negotiated, or when the rabbi makes a decision in religious matters. The diversity in unity can flourish only if it does not threaten the minority opinion, especially if the opinion is expressed by the rabbi. It is impossible to establish and maintain unity as long as one side is "they" (congregation) and the other side is "we", the rabbi and frequently his or her family. I am not familiar with other rabbis' experiences, but I heard more times than it was pleasant, that after the rabbi sincerely answered a question, the reply was, "Yes, you are my rabbi, but..." The division is there and it is to remain there. It makes very little difference whether the division is based on financial differences, or on the question about authority. The rabbi is considered the local authority in matters of religious law, but when the board of directors, or the ritual-religious committee has the authority to override his well-considered and knowledgeable decisions the real issue is how the two parties view each other. It would be ideal if they worked for a consensus instead of viewing each other as belonging to two separate camps, the camp of "we" and the camp of "they", the camp of "yes" and the camp of "yes...but."

PECUNIA V SHEKHINA

(Latin: Money) v. (Hebrew: Dwelling place of God)

As I searched the archives of my congregation, I found one specific operating principle that was in line with my thinking which was prompted by my experience of visiting many synagogues and churches. I have seen the recognition of benefactors' deeds engraved in bronze, copper, marble, and granite. Some reminded me of rows of tombstones that informed the passerby how good were the persons, now sleeping in dust, while walking the earthly paths. In those houses of worship I saw names after names over the doors of rooms spelled in bronze letters, engraved on ritual objects and in decorative calligraphy on framed documents.

I sometimes questioned whether my prayers would be heard in the heavenly heights while standing at the reader's table in the chapel of my previous synagogue. I was struck by the thought that my prayer might have been directed to the spirit of the benefactor who moved to eternal life. Right in front of my eyes on the post of the candelabra engraved was the donor's name.

Previous administrations of my new congregation, especially the ones under whose aegis the new building was erected, made serious decisions. One, included in the operational guidelines of the congregation, prescribed the maintenance of a registry, a book to record each donation with the donor's name, but no plaques of any kind would be allowed anywhere in the building. Only one exception was allowed, the bronze memorial tablet which was transferred from the old synagogue building to one side of the back wall of the new. The plaques on it commemorated the names and dates of death of deceased members or the same data for relatives of members. Anticipating growth in membership led to the consideration to place a similarly designed new tablet on the other side of the back wall. The chairman of the memorial committee was in charge to turn on the memorial lights on the appropriate dates every week.

To me as a survivor of the Holocaust it seemed almost like a duty to install some kind of a reminder of that dark period in the history of European Jewry in the sanctuary. Yad Vashem, the Israel Holocaust Museum commissioned the creation of a suitable light. I initiated the purchase. One family decided to purchase one of those memorial lights and wanted a plaque on the base of the light. I became the center of the dispute. The wisdom of the old policy's initiators prevailed even in this case, and a compromise allowed the placement of a plaque, memorializing the victims of the Nazi terror, near the large bronze tablet.

A few years later, after my retirement someone suggested a purchase of a Tree of Life to be placed on one of the walls in the foyer with the specification that his name will be displayed on a special plaque. The controversy raged for months. The new president argued that the congregation needed the Tree of Life as a fund-raising device, and having a special plaque really would not make much of a difference. In a weak moment against my will I allowed myself to be drawn into the congregational politics when I was asked to offer my opinion as a consultant. I cherished the written guideline and directed the board to the policy that has been adhered to for decades. Although I never thought of myself as a fortune teller or a mind reader, I considered the possible permission as just the first step toward a long series of identical requests. The opponents believed that they had enough power to control any tide in this respect. I was not an advisor, I was called as a consultant, the power to make the final decision rested with the board. The permission was granted.

I have not been in the building for several years since we became members of the other congregation in town. But the loss and the funeral service of a friend took me to the sanctuary. When I arrived, I felt a jolt in my chest. Over the door larger than two-inch-high letters announced the name of a donor after whom the sanctuary was named. I thought that the house of prayer was erected to the glory of God. Then I learned that the glory of men could replace the glory of God. Seeing the dedication, I recalled the conclusion of the memorial services that were held in the donors' home for the first week after his funeral. The liturgy included these words of a Psalm, "People console themselves with the thought that their houses would endure forever and their homes through all generations. So they name their estates after themselves. It is all in vain, humans do not abide in splendor."

A short tour in the rest of the building turned my mind to the serious decision about having a book, listing the donors and their gifts, rather than plaques in the synagogue proper. The chapel, the place for the daily services, bore the name of another departed big donor. The house of study, the classrooms were adorned with more plaques with more names. Similarly was marked the room, the social hall, that served the third role of the synagogue. It was named after a couple who never attended services, but the executor of their will found it fitting to make a contribution and furnish the room in their memory.

I was left with a similar feeling that hit me every time when moved to a new congregation. I mourned to leave behind what we accomplished while living with that group of people.

It was my decision to serve small congregations. In small congregations, the maintenance of the religious school's stability is a serious issue. Ann and I worked hard to organize and reorganize the schools where we lived. Leaving behind the fruit of our work raised sadness, grief, and mourning in my heart.

I cherish the memory of those whose name is not engraved anywhere. Their wisdom has been written in the guideline they left behind. I proudly and joyfully adhered to their advice. But suddenly my joy turned into sadness.

I mourn the death of a policy.

OUT OF THE MOUTHS OF BABES

Step by step I reached self-realization and satisfaction that had been closer to the idea I had in mind. I already made the change. At home, I was still the housewife, but I worked also away from the house. I began teaching, first for no reimbursement, then for a salary. The work was to my liking. My involvement with the teaching in the congregations' schools gave me an opportunity to ease the burden which his varied duties put on my husband. But I set my sight beyond those boundaries. I realized what I was able to do. To widen my scope of expertise, I enrolled in education courses which the local colleges offered. The Jewish Community Center maintained a preschool and had a long time history of being of the highest quality. I approached the director and volunteered to work with the children just prior to their nursery school age. The work was delightful. When one of the teachers decided to move into other areas of work, the director approached me whether I was willing to fill the vacancy. That position took my morning hours. I still could teach the afternoon school classes freeing some time for my husband to meet other responsibilities. As teacher in the nursery school I met non-Jewish children and Jewish boys and girls whose parents were members of our Temple and the other congregation. I was their teacher and at the same time I learned a great deal from them. I might have considered myself a double agent.

One of my added benefits was that I learned things which my husband did not know. He learned English from books and by taking college courses. He was treated with a certain respect, and while speaking with him people watched their tongue. I learned some of my English from the children who brought to school the language spoken on the streets. I remember moments when I talked at home and he did not have the vaguest idea what I was talking about. He said, "yah, that's your kinder-garten language," and with some humor and some regret he said, "I can be a college professor, but I would flunk kindergarten".

I was their teacher. I discharged knowledge and I learned bits and pieces of non-solicited information. I was not a spy, but from their stories an interesting picture developed which revealed an insight to the home life of some congregants.

One day a little girl from my class asked to be excused and did not return after a reasonable time. I asked the teacher's aide to take over the class activities and I began searching for her. I went from room to room and since she was not seen anywhere, I looked into the girls' restroom. No sign of my little one. When I was ready to move back to my class, I saw the door to the boys' bathroom open. There she was. The director and I began talking with her and -as if she had not known- we told her that there was a bathroom for the girls and another for the boys; the girls would go to theirs and the boys to the other.

She looked at us with her eyes wide open and asked, "Why? At home my mommy and daddy use the same bathroom!"

This girl had some gender identity crisis at an early age. She had an older and a younger sister, no brother. One day she came to school wear-ing a baseball cap backwards as many of the boys did. When we ques-tioned her about her fashion statement, she turned to us, "I don't want to be called Debbie, from now on my name is Andrew. I wear my hat this way because my Dad wears it this way, too."

One rainy day, my aide and I decided to read to the class. We selected a story about "My family". The book described usual family events and how the family handled some problems that arose in every day life. All of a sud-den one of the girls jumped to her feet and yelled out, " I will tell you what happened in my family last night. I was sitting in the kitchen, my Mom and Dad had some kind of a fight. My Mom is a strong person. She pushed my Dad out to the porch and quickly locked the door. Dad knocked and knocked, but my Mommy did not let him come in."

We did not want to encourage her to get us involved in her family's affairs. We just kept quiet hoping that the story would soon come to an end. It did. She said, "I don't like arguments. I just picked up myself, went upstairs to my bedroom, and just minded my own business."

Our school enjoyed a good reputation due to the policies which our long-time director had. Many of the non-Jewish families enrolled their young ones in our classes. There was no sign of any discrimination. One day we were hit by a surprise. We were sitting on the floor, playing some game involving everyone. It was some sort of free activity time and our young ones freely socialized. Our attention was drawn to a girl, the daughter of a member of our congregation. She was crying and with downright hostility in her eyes looked at the boy who was sitting on her side. We asked her what was hurting. With tears running down on her cheeks she told us that when she asked Barry to marry her, he said, "I can't marry you, you are Catholic, and I am Jewish." "But believe me, I am really Jewish, I really am, I really am."

Not only my students in school, our children, too, taught us to be careful when it came to language. It has been very common to hear from adult members of our congregations that when their parents did not want them to know what they were discussing, they turned the conversation into Yiddish which they did not understand.

My parents applied the same tactics with me and my younger sister. They spoke Yiddish with the three older ones, but probably gave up on us, the two younger ones. We did not learn the language. As far as I know my husband's parents also spoke Yiddish. He grew up in the Nazi era. He had to take German in school, but at home he refused to speak Yiddish which he considered a derivative of medieval German. When the parents addressed him in Yiddish, he did not answer in that language. Yiddish was not and could not be the medium of our daily conversations. But our children, just as well as we, occasionally were exposed to certain Yiddish words and phrases.

One day, they heard somebody refer to me as the Rabbitzin. They always knew me as Mom, they did not know where to put this new designation.

They decided to turn to us for an explanation. Our younger one came up with the question, "Mom, if Dad is the Rabbi, and you are the Rebbitzin, does it make us the rabbits?"

Since we did not speak Yiddish and made the decision to speak only English and at times Hebrew in our home, it was inevitable that our children overheard some of our conversations. We spoke of a variety of experiences. We discussed celebrations and some details of the events. Our daughter about age eleven, listened intently when we talked about Bar and Bat Mitzvah observances, weddings, and holiday celebration. She absorbed what she heard. One Saturday afternoon she came along to stroll downtown. She loved to look at window displays. She asked us to stop at one of the jewelry store windows. She studied the glitter, the gold, and the diamonds. She learned that she could twist her father around her finger. In her usual manner she pointed at the ring with the largest stone and said, "Daddy, marry me." She knew about marriage, weddings, and wedding rings. She really meant to say, "Daddy, buy me that ring."

Besides students and our own children, our grandchildren opened my eyes and ears to some concepts they held about religion and observances. My cousin, who was responsible for introducing me to my husband, happened to live in the same city where our children and grandchildren lived. At one of our visits with them, I proudly took the oldest of our three grandsons, about two-and-a-half at that time, to see her. While we were there, she repeatedly invited our grandson to give her a kiss. He pretended he did not hear the invitation and did not reply. It was already close to our leaving and he started moving to the door. My cousin gave it another try and asked to give her a kiss. Our little boy was not in the habit of hugging and kissing an almost total stranger. He acted as he could no longer ignore the request. He pushed his back against the door, looked at my cousin straight in her eye, and with the greatest sincerity made his statement, "Jewish people don't kiss."

Our other grandson, his younger brother, also seemed to be very proud of his religious affiliation. They were riding in their van with another couple when one of them asked him a question. He politely and correctly answered with a great smile. His mother, who is not holding back compliments, turned to him and whispered into his ear, "You are cute." He did not take the compliment well. In protest quite loudly he turned to his mother, "I am not cute, I am Jewish."

Which grandmother would not think that her grandchildren are plain genius? I am not an exception. But in my wildest dream I would not have thought that our third grandson at age seven was familiar with Freud.. But his question suggested that he was on the same level as the father of psychoanalysis. In order to complete his theory which he developed in *Moses and Monotheism* about who and what the God of the Jewish people was, Freud accepted the widely known theory at his life time that the Jews' God was a mountain God which frequently erupted.

This grandson was on the way home with his parents from one of the High Holiday services. Apparently he was attentive there and listened to the chanting of the prayers. Apparently two Hebrew words of a confessional prayer, *Avinu Malkeinu* (Our Father, our King), made the greatest impression on him. In a meditative mood he turned to his mother, "Mom, why do we pray to Avinu Volcano?"

To teach and to learn is a statement in the Jewish morning prayer. I taught and some time I learned a very important lesson, a teacher must be eternally vigilant. In the classroom, every moment is extremely important.

In the beginning of winter, the right time for seasonal sniffling, nose blowing, and sneezing, I was working on something and faced the black board on the wall. Suddenly, I felt a little hand stroking my leg. I quickly turned around. A girl stood there with her reddish nose, her two hands on her hips. With an expression of hurt on her face she said, "Mrs. Klein, I sneezed, 'God bless me,' please."

No matter how we loved them, at times it was impossible to acknowledge their every little sound. No matter what, winter, spring, summer, or fall, clouds, or sunshine, the words out of the mouths of those babes warmed my heart. Their pure innocence, straight-forward logic, and open honesty, are gifts that carry no prize tag, their effect is precious and very long lasting.

Learning More Than English–Sign Language

In non-orthodox synagogues men and women sit side by side in the pews. The rabbi, the cantor and some times certain officers of the congregation take their designated seats on the rostrum.

I heard it several times from my family, especially from my wife, how much she would enjoy sitting together at times of prayer the same way as we were at home. It was not for us before I retired from the pulpit.

The world looks very different from the heights of the pulpit than it does from the pews. One of my colleagues put this experience eloquently in an e-mail message posted on our listserve, "[This medium] gives us all the chance to 'be', to ventilate, not to be judged by colleagues…but to be loved unconditionally for the very fact that we walk a lonely path in the arid forest of disenchantment and disillusionment. We need each other…"

Besides our colleagues this statement includes especially our spouses. The Bible says that God created Eve to be an equal helping partner to Adam. Being a congregational rabbi, I realized how much truth was in this statement.

In a moment of disenchantment and disillusionment half jokingly, but more than half seriously not without any 'chutzpah' I drew a cartoon and in the caption expressed my opinion, "instead of a sermon, I always want to say something.'

While 'saying something' I was not always sure that the 'special something' was heard by the congregation. But, as if in the shadow of the pulpit, behind which I was conducting services or delivering a sermon, my wife, sitting in the pews, used a device she developed throughout the years. Her signals warned me that I said something louder than necessary, and instructed to lower my voice, or to straighten out my necktie, or to stand straight instead of stooped, or just to watch the people in the pews.

The sign language was like a road sign, telling us that we were on a two-way street. She signaled me gently. The signals which I devised might have not been as pleasant as the ones she sent me. Sometimes I sent a signal, a nod of the head with the message that I appreciated a reminder, and sent my love. But more often it expressed my expectation of my wife and our children. Outsiders frequently remarked about my bushy eye brows, our family trademark. The insiders, my family, remarked about my eyes under the eye brows. The signals they sent were like shooting arrows that expressed my displeasure when either the children or my wife broke the laws of decor and discipline by talking to the persons on the right or the left, or behaviorally expressing an opinion about the length of the sermon or the service by fidgeting. To me it was not acceptable that my family members behaved like some of the congregants. I expected proper and dignified behavior from every member of my family.

The sign language has been a tool that marked a change in our relationship. In the early years of our marriage, my wife was my sounding board. Either because I had to be sure how I expressed myself in English or because of my perfectionist attitude, I have never ascended the pulpit without a complete text of whatever I planned to say. Before that time arrived, in the privacy of our home I asked her to sit with me and listen to whatever I prepared. It was stroking and soothing to hear that she liked what she heard. But after a while I was not so sure that I could rely on my critique. Whatever to her sounded wonderful, the audience did not always hear it the same way. Many times, the reaction was flat and unenthusiastic. This experience prompted me to express my desire that rather than speaking words of love and admiration, I needed true criticism. After making this request repeatedly, my wife began awakening and stepping out of the shadow offering critical remarks. She reacted similarly to the arrows that were shot at her from my strict and dictatorial eyes. She told me that she wanted to be herself rather that a slavish follower of instructions.

The signs that substituted for verbal expressions were not expressions of affection all the times, Ann considered them a way just to stay in contact even if the pulpit separated me from the pews.

I appreciated this means of communication with Ann and the children when all of us were still living together, but it had assumed much greater significance when our children left home. They were not sitting on their mother's side. Ann's feeling of the empty nest syndrom was carried from the home to the synagogue. It was part of the realization that we arrived at the same point where we were in the beginning, just the two of us.

Not exactly. There was a result of my request for expressing criticism. Our children went to school, completed their education, established their own homes, and became, thankfully, successful in their chosen professions. They learned a way to look at me. Now I find myself facing criticism about many of my thoughts and behaviors. Another phrase entered our conversations, 'thank you I stand corrected' whether I believe it is necessary or not. I do say it lovingly. The way we established our communication, it became open, honest, intimate and accepting. There is hardly a day that I would not think of them, our relationship with them, our appreciation for them, and for the acceptance with which we relate to each other.

We were young when we started. Had no previous education, we had no opportunity to take courses on parenting, we grew up with our children. When our grandchildren came, I became a much better parent. We worked hard to give them the freedom to become themselves.

Learning is a mutual experience. As insignificant as it seems, one day I had a meaningful experience when one of our married children was ready to leave, my wife eagerly asked, 'when will you come home again?' to which the reply was, 'Mom, I have my home, I come here to visit.'

This was an expression of freedom. All of us know that whatever we learned from verbal and non-verbal communication became a building block in our total relationship.

BUILD A SANCTUARY THAT I MAY DWELL AMIDST THEM

I loved our sanctuary. Before my classes began, I walked in there. It was my favorite time of the day. I was not the wife of the rabbi. I was not the teacher. I did not have an assigned seat. I sat in the last row alone. The wheels of my mind started turning and when they stopped I fell into a meditative mood. At times I looked at the biblical quotation fixed on the mantle over the Ark, "Build a Sanctuary that I May Dwell Amidst Them."

I felt calm sitting there alone, but on occasion I felt the pain of many experiences. I wondered whether the divine justice dwelt in the heart of people. Not once I looked at the words and wondered whether we allowed God to dwell in our midst. I thought of criticism.

I remembered the days when my husband came home and told me about the critical remarks which the man, the member of our congregation, made on Thursdays while reviewing his sermons to improve them. He was happy with that criticism. It was intended to be constructive, helpful, to increase his knowledge and efficiency. He talked to me about other types of criticism, too, the destructive ones that assassinate the character, that destroy self esteem and confidence.

At the time when I was fearful that my children would look at me as if I were illiterate, the slightest critical remark cut into my flesh, bones, and soul. I did not trust myself. The only way I knew to counter the critical remarks was defensiveness. I knew how much it took me to climb out of my frightened self and learned not to allow the venom of critical remarks to define me.

I sat there in the stillness of the sanctuary thinking how my husband felt when he heard congregants' criticism which sounded more destructive than constructive. I wondered how he felt when a congregant wrote a letter to the board and called him a rotten apple which spoiled the apple cart.

Luckily not all criticism was like that. Somebody left a message for him in the office while he visited shut-ins in the hospital. He just returned to start his class and could not return the call immediately. While teaching, the same person called again. When Joel finally had the few minutes needed to return the call, unexpectedly harsh words were hurled at him, "It is easier to reach the president of the United States than you." Is justice in the heart of people?

I hoped that he had strong armor to protect himself from the pain of the wounds that these dart- like statements caused on his soul. Thinking of myself and my husband, I knew that one person could not satisfy everybody, I still hoped that what we were giving would be appreciated by many if not all. I knew how hard Joel worked. I knew how strong my support intended to be. Only I knew that he was ready any day any time to be available to those who needed him. He worked in that style because he wanted to with the knowledge that not everybody appreciated his effort.

I sat in the last row of seats and thought of the story I read once about two New York men who walked together every morning to the train station. On the way they stopped at the newspaper vendor's stand, and while waiting for his paper, one of them usually asked the vendor with genuine interest how he was, how he felt selling his papers in the cold of the winter and on the heat of sunny summer days. The reply came every time in the same tone that expressed that he took the question as an intrusion into his privacy.

After the man got his paper, they continued walking. Once the companion asked why his colleague still bothered to ask. He replied, "I continue asking him because I am interested to know how he was. His reaction does not dictate how I behave." This story deeply affected me and my behavior.

I questioned myself. Did I do justice to myself that I allowed critical remarks to cast a shadow over words of appreciation that I heard throughout the years? I easily dismissed the words of appreciation which I earned for my efforts. I forgot the appreciation and admiration for my insistence to improve and introduce change. I did not think of my mother's recipes that helped me to produce dinners which I served before board meetings held in our home. I received sincere appreciation for the atmosphere that surrounded the guests who liked to dine with us.

I recall the result of my decision to acquire the skill to chant the Haftarot. It was not easy to learn the traditional tune for these biblical chapters that conclude the scripture portion of the service. I used many of my free hours and occasional opportunities to refine my skills. Knowing how phobic Joel was on bridges and high altitudes, crossing Tappan Zee Bridge on the way to Camp Ramah in the Poconos, where I worked a few summers, I took the High Holiday prayer book and practiced the chanting of the portion about the birth of Samuel. At the end of the summer I chanted this portion at the service. I was the first woman in the congregation who was allowed to act in this role. I received words of praise and encouragement.

My love to teach earned similar remarks. I offered Hebrew reading courses for adults several times. My love resounded in the people who signed up for the course.

Although it is par for the course that at times unjust criticism is our reward, it is difficult to keep events in the right perspective. It is difficult to become vulnerable in the face of unjust criticism. My strong side is my ability to relate to people. I could go out with a number of women in the congregation, I could play cards and other social games with others, but there were only a few with whom to be friends, to cry, to laugh, to celebrate, and to mourn. I was able to establish lasting friendships in every community where we lived. But in my experience we became friends with people who were members of the congregations which we had left. These relationships provided me, not as a person, but as the rabbi's wife, with important lessons. They became our friends in whom I could confide; whom I could trust "to 'be' and not be judged", not to fear that their knowledge of my personal issues might influence them to stand with us, behinds us, or against us when the issue was our life and livelihood.

WHERE I STOOD

In 1975, two years before negotiation about the renewal of my contract were to come up, I went through a thorough soul searching to see what effects my twenty-eight years as a congregational rabbi had on me, my thinking, my feelings, in one word on my life.

In this country I served only smaller congregations. In my experience attendance at services and all functions was always higher while the honeymoon between the new rabbi and the congregation lasted. As soon as the newness wore off, congregants returned to their regular habits. I found they had no genuine interest in regular prayer services.

In order to bring people to services special occasions had to be created. I worked at creating them since frequently the signs of Jewishness were seen in the number of people who sat in the pews. But I know of no producer who could create a new show and attraction every week, not to speak of every day. I saw myself in a realistic light, I am not a producer. I knew that I was a better rabbi in the living room than on the height of the pulpit. In all congregations where I served the adult study groups were attracting more people than the regular prayer services with the exception of the High Holidays.

Aside from the attitudes and practices of congregants and fellow-Jews, first and foremost I wanted to find an answer to how my religious observance, attitudes to God, revelation, and Jewish law were altered since I was ordained.

After completing my studies at the seminary, my religious observance was influenced by teachers of our traditional codes. My professors claimed to be progressive, but in reality they were ardent opponents of free thinking. Observance to them and to me meant a strict adherence to the letter

121

of the law and even a condemnation of those who chose dissent and attempted to follow different ways. Living a number of years in the congregational setting, my observance was directed by freedom of choice. In my case that meant a search for personal fulfilment by following the spirit and intent rather than the letter of the law. I reexamined my Hungarian neolog model that, even after World War II, opposed the introduction of any prayers in the vernacular. The sermon delivered in Hungarian was considered to be the main expression of our commitment to the culture in which we were rooted.

At ordination time I accepted the idea of God that was taught by my teachers who tried to interpret writings of philosophers. My own God idea grew out of search, understanding, and perception. It matured from the childish look. My attitude toward God was the result of cognitive development. It was not the fear of parents projected into the supernatural. It was a desire to follow the inspiration that moves me to become more and more like the ideals I attributed to the divine. Studying the history of our people in depth, I discovered long forgotten, intentionally and unintentionally altered facts and arrived at a God-idea that developed throughout the centuries in the minds of the Jewish people and in the thinking of others. I defined the limits or limitlessness of my God and God-idea. It expanded with knowledge and did not shrink by gaining new information.

I viewed revelation as a process. The Torah, the first known constitution of our people, records that there was more than one revelation. I believe that the Torah had been composed initially and amended several times in a theocracy where its final authority was rooted in God. For me it does not mean that the Torah was spoken by the One that it is unchangeable and remains eternally the same from the first generation to the last. I do not believe that it is the truth which was handed down to us and we ought to make every effort to prove that it is the truth. I strive to discover truth as the end result of inquiry.

As the next natural step, I examined my attitude toward Jewish law. In Hungary I served on the rabbinic committee which had the authority to give answers to inquiries about the appropriate application of our laws to every-day life. In the United States, as a member of the Rabbinical Assembly, I aspired to serve on the Committee on Jewish Law and Standards. When I was granted that honor, I went to our meetings with my respect for tradition which I considered to be similar to a trunk of a tree that gives supporting nourishment to the constantly sprouting new branches. I expressed my belief in line with my understanding of revelation that men formulated law to control human instincts. Therefore men must have the right to consider law in the light of the ever-changing conditions. My remarks were based on my belief that religion is a break on instincts, but it should not be allowed to become the shackle on human life. I opposed a religion that can be used as an oppressing force which inflicts suffering by its authority. I want my religion to direct man to live fully and to allow life's joy to flow freely. I do not value asceticism as a virtue, but strive for wholesomeness that allows total living.

These views did not always become sources of great satisfaction in my congregational rabbinate. I began my service with the belief that I was a leader by the position which my office afforded me with. I believed that I was given the power and authority to direct. But in later years I came to realize that a source of satisfaction had not been the position of leadership authority but the opportunity to make contact with a great variety of people in "leadership" capacity. At the descent from the peak of my career the real source of satisfaction was the rare discovery that I had left a mark in the thinking, life-style, and perception of some people, especially the younger elements which will become future policy makers.

As a rabbi I derived the least satisfaction from the lack of response to my sincere suggestions that we have the freedom to make decisions about our religious observance. I was really disappointed with the uncritical repetition of ceremonies and rituals that were accepted and honored as the most ancient, authentic, and genuine tradition, although they were not even practiced earlier than the life time of our generation's grandparents.

At that reflection time I examined also the synagogue whose rabbi I was. I searched my mind and soul whether I would participate in the programs and the religious services it conducted if I were not its rabbi. I concluded that I could not be part of a rote repetition of prayers and attend programs on such elementary level that was below my interest. But I was not sure how I communicated my values and ideas to my congregation. I was not clear whether my sermons played any role to imply the alternatives I preferred.

In a conscious effort, for years I gave up sermonizing. Since it was expected, I delivered four sermons a year on the High Holidays. Even those were not sermons in the generally accepted sense. I could not follow the model for sermons I received in my seminary training. It ran against my grains to twist a biblical verse or a quote to present it as the foundation of a thought I wanted to communicate. I initiated several alternatives. I attempted to make every service topical with a point of concern. Even if we used the regular prayer book, my concern was to make the services innovative. I placed great emphasis on lay participation in every aspect of the service. I enjoyed an open dialogue between the pulpit and the pew, either in the form of "Ask the rabbi" or "Ask the congregation." I applied this format to the Torah reading which became an open-ended study period with congregants freely asking questions or verbalizing their thoughts. We assigned a previously agreed upon topic for discussion during the social period following services. Instead of formal services sometimes we prayed around festival dinner tables. Other times we moved the services from the synagogue to private homes. Since in an age of telespots and short messages I could not justify and demand attention to long discourses and monologues, we had a short presentation either by the rabbi, or a male or female congregant.

I welcomed the Law Committee's decision to accept women's participation in every aspect of Jewish living. I worked for its implementation long before the decision was made public. I was gratified to see it in practice although it was not wholeheartedly supported by some men—even those in power—but it was taking hold slowly. Some women attended the regular weekday morning and evening services, and were granted *aliyot*. Ann's willingness and insistence resulted in a woman chanting the Haftarah for the first time on Rosh Hashanah.

These small but significant changes added freshness and liveliness to our gatherings, but I was aware that it did not come from a genuine devotion to prayer in the soul.

So I queried if I were given *carte blanche*, what changes would I have wanted to implement in my ideal synagogue's educational, religious and youth programs.

Since I do not see how the present ideology would convince our people to hold onto our Jewishness outside Israel, my answer was and is that if it were up to me, I would revamp the programming and build it on a different ideology. I would orient all synagogue programs to show how Jewish folk-ways and ethnicity developed into a religious system. On this basis I would probe the meaning of Jewishness on every level and make people see why it is worth living our separateness differently from our Christian-influenced understanding of religion.

Soul searching and self-questioning was part of my service, but when I put these thoughts into writing, the greatest challenge confronting my congregation and me was simply existence. On the local scene merger talks were conducted with the Center and the Reform congregation. I saw that our group faced the possibility and reality of being swallowed up into a new Reform organization where the defunct Conservative Temple's members would never be accepted as equals or equal partners in the new organization. Apart from this local problem, I saw finances as a great challenge caused by the ever-decreasing number of members and the lack of true interest in the synagogue way. I saw that a great number of Jews had no sense of need for it, thus no sense of obligation. The non-affiliated represented a third, probably the largest congregation in our community. Their number has been and is on the increase. Many of the affiliated hold that as long as the synagogues are already here it is good to have them, but it should not require extra effort to maintain it. We are void of the necessary atmosphere that could present an ideological challenge to define to which synagogue one would belong.

After my decision to retire from the rabbinate, we remained citizens of the community. Without having any sense of telling the future, in my view the religious leadership is being replaced by a secular one, and this struggle had been the underlying factor of the merger talks to bring the existing Jewish organizations under one roof.

The concluding thoughts in my soul searching raised the issue how my position as a congregational rabbi has posed special problems with regard to my wife, our children and our home life.

The answers to this question are found in the stories and anecdotes, scattered throughout this writing. They reflect on living in the shadow of the pulpit.

AFTER THIRTY YEARS

Long before the merger mania of commercial enterprises began, some of the Jewish leaders in our community began talking about the future of the three local organizations.

This new development had a lasting effect on our lives. It is my hope that I can enlighten the reader about this development by providing some background information as I was aware of it at that time.

One of the institutions–involved in the merger plans–was the Jewish Community Center. It grew out of the old settlement house that served the immigrant community well. The others were the synagogues. The largest, the reform congregation was the heir of the orthodox Litvische Schul. The smaller which was established by mostly Russian immigrants as another orthodox synagogue, adopted a new name–identical with three other temples' in the State–and affiliated with the conservative movement, but continued–at least in nostalgic remembrance–the 'sfard' tradition, as it has been interpreted by its old-timers.

The larger congregation in the middle of the 50s decided to erect a new building and move from the street where both synagogues were located about one block away from each other. The smaller congregation made an identical decision and by moving to its new location it enlarged the distance between the two temples to at least seven blocks. The rabbi of the larger congregation did not agree with the reform affiliation and was invited to serve the conservative group. Having been orthodox, he was comfortable with the unchanged manners of the prayer services in that synagogue, but did not go along with the mixed seating of the conservative practice when later it was introduced. He decided to leave the pulpit and became the head of an orthodox day school in another state.

Both congregations hired new rabbis. But the old country traditions continued. The first generation immigrants and their growing families continued the attitude that became a tradition. The orthodox Litvische Schule, now turned reform, considered itself superior to the other both in educational and financial respects. The rabbis of the two congregations, either for their own ideological orientation, or for reasons of survival, joined in this evaluation nurturing the separation and keeping the distance between the two groups.

With this background came the idea of merging the three organizations in order to ease the financial burdens in the 1970s. They considered the elimination of duplications by combining first the schools which the two congregations operated separately, then combining the administration of the three existing organizations under one roof, and finally forming the largest congregation in the State by abandoning one building and joining the services of the two congregations.

Some of the business-minded people supported the plan for logical reasons. The difference in the level of observance of both congregations' members was insignificant. At a rough count, probably there were more kosher homes in the reform congregation than in the conservative. The enthusiasm for the merger was fueled by the hope that by the merger the sustained antagonistic attitude would disappear and all members would be accepted on the higher level of prestige.

If the merger were accomplished, one congregation needed only one rabbi. But at that time there were two in office. Seeking a solution, first the reform congregation voted not to renew the contract of their rabbi. The conservative congregation, either on the conscious or unconscious level, became concerned of the possibility that history would repeat itself and their more traditional rabbi would become an obstacle to the merger by emphasizing the differences between the two ideological approaches to Jewish religious life. There were voices that put weighty emphasis on the rabbi's more traditional approach. A campaign began without consulting him about his stand on the merger issue. For others his more traditional thinking and practice did not represent a weighty issue enough to defeat the renewal of his contract. Some of these people resorted to smear campaigns, going as far as to spread their opinion that the rabbi lied about his academic credentials. They organized meetings outside the temple organization to discuss the strategy.

When I heard about these activities, I dismissed them since I strongly believed that the truth would prevail, and anyway some of the campaign leaders were already known as "rabbi killers" who opposed any religious leader on principle.

As hurting as the experience was, I came to learn some interesting sidelines of which I would not have thought otherwise. During my tenure with the congregation, like all rabbis, I was called upon to consult and approached to assist in troublesome circumstances. The difficulties might have involved domestic issues, parent child relationships, a member getting entangled with legal issues, someone arrested, others imprisoned. Performing the duties of my office, I complied. I never thought that my assistance might be turned against me in any connection. At the time when the vote on my contract was taken, it became an issue. I arrived at a conclusion that people generally do not like and do not want to have witnesses to their difficulties. A number of no votes came from many of those who turned to me for help.

Another experience brought a smile to my face. More properly it could have been taken for a grin. After the votes were tallied, one member came to see me and made the following statement, "Rabbi, I voted against the renewal of your contract because after all the years you were with us, you deserved a life-time contract, and they would not grant it to you." (Probably one can get through a life time without having friends of this kind).

The events of the merger moved along two fronts. The most important issue was not whether my contract was renewed or not. A small group of staunch supporters of the reform separateness did not want to see the "Russische Schul" become part of that congregation. They firmly believed in the initial thoughts and principles that began the movement in

Germany. They did not want more Hebrew in the services. They opposed the request that the students wear a head covering for sacred studies and prayer in school. They wanted to defeat the merger on some legal principles so badly that they provided financial support to the opposition within the conservative group.

The reform rabbi was reinstated, his contract was renewed, the conservative rabbi's contract was not. Unreasonably or not, I suffered significant psychological damage. As it was known to my family, but not always appreciated by others, I was a devoted rabbi. I felt defeated and angry. The public knowledge of our plan, that we wanted to make this city our permanent home, created the assumption that we would accept conditions even if they were disadvantageous for us during the previous contract negotiations.

That statement haunted me again. The vote proved that it was our mistake for the second time. We decided to stay, but for months it was difficult. I could not set foot in the conservative temple. If I felt the need for joining a prayer quorum, I took off and went to a different community.

After several months I was able to overcome my anger and hurt and occasionally went back to services.

On one occasion insult was added to injury. At the morning services I was offered an honor. At the end of the service, a board member who was among the leaders of the campaign against the renewal of my contract very loudly expressed his opposition to giving me an honor because I was not a member of the congregation. I continued living in the community. For some reason, unknown to me, the president of the congregation offered us honorary membership in the congregation. The honor was short-lived. The next president decided to terminate the offer.

The congregation went through hard times. First the conservative rabbinic placement office refused to recommend candidates because financial issues were pending between me and the congregation. Instead of resolving those issues, the congregation placed advertisements in Jewish papers. They elected rabbis with no credentials. One probably did not have even

Jewish credentials. Another disappeared before his officiating duties commenced. In the midst of the difficulties another leader of the smear campaign, who then served as the chair of the ritual committee, phoned me. Since they had nobody who could read the Torah on Saturday, he asked whether I would do the "honor" as a great help to the congregation. I cannot identify whether it was my sarcasm that glossed over my anger, or my arrogance, that I replied curtly saying that 'I was a package deal.'

While my silent struggle was going on, life moved on. I worked on the realization of my childhood desire to do work in the field of psychology. I studied, passed examinations, worked as a marriage and family therapist, earned the rank of approved supervisor of training for marriage and family therapy, met the requirements for certification as a sex counselor, and for a while became a state certified psychologist.

By chance, I had met a young catholic priest, while still serving my congregation. He opened a new horizon for me and moved me to lend an ear to what he was saying. He invited me to join a training and support group for clergy. I joined while I pursued supervision in the field of family therapy.

The steps I began to take brought about something that was entirely new to me. As a Jew and as a rabbi with a European background, I felt like an outsider in the Christian environment. The feeling was somewhat familiar, I was an outsider in the Jewish community, too. With our approach to observance, our family was part of a minority. Many congregants and non-congregants somehow believed that conversing with me they had to talk about religion as if there were no other subjects. At gatherings, some people would not sit at a table with us because they felt restricted by our mere presence. When as a clergy I was invited to "deliver an invocation or benediction" I felt like, in the phrase a colleague once coined, one of the "book ends at the extremes on the dais."

While a chaplain consultant in our State Hospital, my good fortune led me into the accepting and embracing arms of a budding pastoral therapist group. Up to that point, I did not know anything about pastoral counseling or pastoral psychotherapy. Our school did not prepare us for this role, consciously and/or structurally including courses in our curriculum. This group of protestant ministers became my representatives of religious orientation and soon a religious experience for me. I attended our weekly peer meetings with a fervor of religious practice, and, having experienced a period of hard times with the local Jewish congregational life, the group became my "adopting and adopted Church."

I enlisted and became a soldier to serve, and contribute to the uphill efforts for certification as pastoral counselors in our state. My previous experiences did not arm me with enough finesse and political savvy to make—what I believed to be—meaningful contributions. I looked at me as the enlisted man among the commissioned officers. I felt a need to contribute to such an extent that my friends, my peers, counseled me about what they termed 'my neediness.'

The soldier grew in the battle. The very young imperfect certification law underwent a revision that required fellow level membership in the American Association of Pastoral Counselors which I did not have. I was aware of my abilities, the quality of my work, and the years of psychotherapy experience behind me. Still when I looked at the Association's Membership Directory, I could find hardly ten rabbis listed nationwide. I questioned how I, the Jew, would become a member on that higher level in such an illustrious and homogeneous protestant organization.

Helping hands were extended and accepted. My peer group encouraged and trained me to take the leap. I applied for the fellow level membership; the paperwork was approved. The time for the personal screening interview approached rapidly. A few members of my consulting group formed a committee that invited me for a mock interview. One of my colleagues—with his best intentions—remarked to encourage me, "The regional committee will not approve you just because you are a rabbi, you will have to work for it." I do not know with what the road to hell is paved. Some people say it is good will. That remark did not sound like the good will to encourage me. It was like the centrifugal force. It put me in a spin and I felt like I was orbiting somewhere on the periphery of christian society.

The regional committee evaluated my interview and submitted its approval to the national organization whose final action accepted me as a fellow.

Probably no one under normal circumstances kept any door closed for me, only I did not see the doors open. While being a congregational rabbi, many doors opened automatically just by recognition of the title that was attached to the office I held. At this new phase of my life, I recognized that I, the person, had to turn the knob of those doors to gain entry. I know that I had a respectable reputation with new credentials added to it, fellow of American Association of Pastoral Counselors, fellow of the NH. Psychological Association, clinical member and approved supervisor in American Association for Marriage and Family Therapy, sex counselor certified by the American Association of Sex Educators, Counselors, and Therapists. From the inception of the local Pastoral Counseling Center, I became part of it for several years as a member of its Board of Directors, and later as a senior staff member. These achievements strengthened my feeling of being accepted and enhanced my confidence and trust to belong.

The new opportunities led to the realization of a dream from my high school years on a new level. I did learn a second language in which I was not only able to deliver talks in the profession of my first training, and at that time I was able to present lectures and workshops in the line of a second career. Looking back at my life, fifty plus years as a rabbi of which thirty years were in congregational service on two continents, and the years in private practice as a psychotherapist, I see that I am blessed. I have been able to incorporate my life's trials, tribulations, tributes, and achievements into an integrated outlook and a guiding philosophy. I gained an optimistic view that I could accomplish what I learned in my young adulthood studies about the unification of the functions of body and soul. This view gave me a force as if it was the fulfilment of what we pray for on our holiest days "not to be abandoned when feeble age gives way, and not to be forsaken when our intellectual abilities begin to fade."

FROM THE ALLEY TO THE HILLTOP

After thirty years on the pulpit Joel decided to retire from the rabbinate and did not seek another congregation. He began pursuing his long time desire to work as a psychologist. His decision meant that feelings of loneliness awaited me again.

We meditated and hesitated. We agreed that as the first step into the field of psychology he would pursue certification as a marriage and family therapist. He engaged in serious studies. The field of psychotherapy changed in the thirty years he was away from it. He had to pass exams and became certified also as a psychologist. He needed office space.

Our children were already married, our home, which he designed, was larger than the two of us needed. To have as low an overhead as possible, we agreed to use the study for his office, and the anteroom area for me to work as his receptionist. This arrangement enabled us to separate our private quarters from his workplace. But I was unhappy with the inconveniences this arrangement caused. I was deprived from my private suntanning area in our spacious backyard. The Temple building was just on the other side of the alley. The living fence of bushes did not provide a barrier to the inquisitive eyes. My movements in and around the house were restricted not to disturb the needed quiet and assure that no intrusion would hinder his work.

I was not happy with the functionality of our home from the first time we moved in and had some very definite ideas of what I wanted. Coincidences happen to solve problems frequently. I began looking for a location that I wanted our new home to be. Joel was amicable and he liked the possibility of relocation. He even found it very appealing. He told me how sad he was as a young child when the fascist ordinances confiscated the piece of land his parents owned because it was Jewish property. Then came the communist regime which did not recognize the right of individuals to own property. My suggestion was exciting, we planned to retain our home as an office building and buy a new home, we would own two pieces of property. A real estate agent called me that she knew of a home that would be placed on the market in two days, she wanted me to see it. I drove with her. We went from the alley, where I house was located, to the top of the hill, where the prospective new home was located. I stepped in the house. It was as if someone designed it from a plan I drew up. When we wanted to buy something, we usually had some definite ideas. Even when we bought cars, it did not take more than a half-an hour to close the deal. I called Joel, and asked whether he could come with me to see a house during his lunch time. We went, negotiated, and left the agent. He still had time to have his noon-time meal.

I kept referring to our prospective new home as my dream home, our doll house. In two weeks we closed the purchase and moved. Joel was left with the dull and tedious work of remodeling our old residence. He had to endure the inconvenience of renovating and relocating his office to the first floor area. Our pride just rose to higher levels. Not only did we have two properties, we became landlords. We rented out the second floor and the ground floor became his office. I probably was as happy with this arrangement as with the American state and church separation. I was separated from my husband's business.

While these events took place in our private lives, the community combined the schools of the two congregations in a newly organized Hebrew school and advertised for a director. Having been available, I submitted my application. I was invited for an interview. I felt the butterflies in my stomach. When all the questions were answered, I looked around at the members of the Education Committee. There were some familiar and some unfamiliar faces. The butterflies flew away, but my stomach was in knots. The representative of the conservative congregation, of whom I knew that despite his claim to be our friend voted for the non-renewal of

Joel's contract, looking straight in my eyes, said, "Thank you, we shall notify you of our decision." It seemed that the fate of my application was sealed. I did not get the job. Someone, fifty miles away became the school's first director.

I was offered a few jobs, but all involved working either on every Saturday or on an alternative basis on weekends. I wanted to work. I overcame my pride and apprehension and applied for a teaching position in the Community Hebrew School. It was an unhappy choice. The classes were held in the reform temple building. Different approaches to observance were hardly tolerated, there was no question about whose dominance was evident. The teachers were almost without exception volunteers. In my opinion, the discipline left much to be desired. I became increasingly unhappy since I did not seem to reach the goals I set for my teaching. Frequently I questioned my ability to reach the students. I turned against myself and after an unhappy year, I did not return to the school.

Coincidence and coincidence. At this time, a childhood friend of my husband, the rabbi of the community fifteen miles away was close to his retirement age and asked me whether I would take over some of his teaching responsibilities as a part-time position. He was delighted that I accepted the position and freed him at least partially from his teaching duties in the school. I could not fill the role of Joel's receptionist- typist-accountant any longer. I had my own job, independently from Joel's work.

The years passed. The rabbi retired. The population of the town and the school grew. The congregation had to find the proper accommodation for the growing student body. Some dedicated members of the congregation offered the land, some others engaged in a successful fund raising, and a brand-new school building was erected in front of my eyes. The school committee's chairperson approached me and said that the school's growth required hiring a principal. Just a word was needed, if I wanted the job, it was mine.

My efforts improved the school curriculum and the quality of the teaching staff. My work was appreciated. I grew just as the school grew. I felt fulfilled. I saw the result of my independent work. The external reflection of my inner uncertainties, my old shy withdrawn behavior, turned me into the extravert person who really I am.It was a new territory to conquer. The job presented numerous challenges. But it was like the saying, "you get what you paid for." In the past I paid, and it was time to get paid.

It was a coincidence. I was without a job, the offer seemed acceptable. I became a commuter. I saw the growth of the school. Half of the days were mine. I was away from home only in the afternoons and a few nights of a month to attend the necessary meetings. It was a pleasure to become part of a professional group. I joined professional organizations, attended their meetings and conventions. I turned my volume control to the highest notch and listened to the colleagues' remarks, reports, and the conversations with other school directors. It was like the beginning of my American life. When I learned a new word in English, I could hardly wait to use and practice it. If I learned something new at these meetings, and it fit into the general ideas I had about my job, I gave it a chance and incorporated into my practice.

The difficulties of the job strengthened our marriage. Joel had the experience, I had the trust. I was convinced that I could turn to him to consult or to ask for advice any time. Some of the evenings, and certainly our longer car rides, became the times when I could pick his brain. We became partners in my enterprise. As I stood on his side when he was on the pulpit, he was my support when I sat in the director's chair. I can confidently say that I grew into the job.

It would not have been a congregation, a committee, or a group of parents, if there were no criticism. But I got much less of it than the praises and thanks I earned. I learned that I could stay and operate on my own power. With a growing conviction, I began climbing out of the hole which I dug for myself in my uncertainties. I got used to operating in bright light, out of the shadow which I believed the pulpit cast on me. Not only my fear, which I experienced when I compared myself with other wives of rabbis was waning, but my relationship with rabbis while working for them was reinforcing my confidence. The congregation changed rabbis twice while I was directing the school. Both had their own ideas about running the school, both brought their own education and traditions. They wanted to impose their ideas on me sometimes gently sometimes with more force. I knew that people generally, including my husband, valued my ability to relate to people very highly. Here I was tested. I stood the test and succeeded becoming a consensus builder.

The series of coincidences continued. The new use of our remodeled building as Joel's professional office turned some interest toward us. An offer came from a physician to buy our property. We were not sure about the seriousness of the offer but recalled that the same person some years before mentioned that if we ever decide to sell he wanted to have the first option to make an offer. One night after dinner we got together and without much ceremony the offer was made and accepted.

This completed the dissolution of the fading shadow. Joel happened to find office space to rent on a hilltop at the other side of the city.

At the time of this change another important change affected us. I had surgery and the catholic chaplain paid a visit with me. I introduced him to my husband and they were talking about the changes in our lives. A few weeks later he invited Joel to become part of a clergy support group. It was an important step for him. He reconnected with the local clergy although in a different capacity than before when he was a member of the clergy association. I knew that he had a hard time to remain in touch with them when he left the pulpit. A few years after he joined the support group the same priest suggested to him to use his education, training, and experience in a new capacity. His suggestion was that he could offer a different kind of relationship to his clients if he considered himself a pastoral counselor, later known as pastoral psychotherapist rather than a psychologist. He took this suggestion seriously.

Musings of the Educator

Just about a decade ago I completed forty years of my involvement with Jewish education. It was like the mid-life of my teaching career. I felt a desire to convey in writing what that time meant for me and how I saw Jewish children and their parents in the light of my accumulated experiences.

Looking over my files, I found the script in which I summarized my thoughts which I put in one simple word, admiration.

Further elaborating on this one word, I added that every child is an unfinished product. What makes a child admirable is the vast potential for growth and development. This potential puts the words of wonder on the adults' lips when they hear the child's first word, watch the first step, listen to the first reading, being amazed by the first signs of retention and comprehension. In other words, every action of a child—however insignificant—is an indication of the almost limitless possibilities he or she possesses.

In my decades of teaching and directing Jewish education, I learned to admire my students' abilities and enthusiasm. I have been and I continue to be with them. I look at them and daily become amazed. They go through a strenuous schedule. As the late afternoon hours approach, they slow down and precisely at that time of the day, they come to their Hebrew and Religious studies. They are frequently tired, yet they work. The hours available to them for the classes are few. Not everything can be accomplished while they are in the presence of their teacher. Homework is necessary and inevitable. Almost without exception, the parents of my students have been and are supportive, but many a time, this is the only thing they can provide, their support.

In our country a few decades ago attitudes toward Jewish religious education changed. The horizon opened and widened. We want to have a wider scope of knowledge than just a canned, mechanical performance on one appointed day (Bar Mitzvah celebration). In the past even that was the duty and privilege of only the male students. Now we want equal opportunities and equal education for our daughters. But many of those parents, who enthusiastically provide for the religious education of their children now, did not have the opportunity to be exposed to it when they were in their young years. So our children do their homework on their own; if they run into any difficulty, at times reluctantly, phone the teacher or rely on their classmates.

With these thoughts in mind I made another life style changing decision.

As much as I loved my work in the school, after ten years the commute became increasingly tiring. I started feeling the years. The growing number of meetings kept me away from home into the late hours of the days. The harsh winter with its snow storms lowered my visibility. I did not want to see far ahead in the future. I could not. But I was not ready to give up what I liked to do.

I took a risky step. The idea came from my realizations that I could do the job. The decision, which I made seemed appropriate also for another reason. The Jewish community in our town had grown. The economic conditions changed the composition of the population. The once blooming industrial center suffered a tremendous blow in the early 1960s. More than two dozen factories closed their doors. Many workers lost their jobs and moved to other states. The executives established homes in warmer climates. A period of stagnation was followed by an influx of a transiting white-color workforce. The instability and diminishing general interest in organized religion and organized Jewish education resulted in a growing number of unaffiliated families. The largest congregation in our community was the non-affiliated. I felt a missionary zeal. The temples required membership in order to provide children with a Jewish education in the community school. Material reasons kept some families in the ranks of the non-affiliated. It pained me that young children of those families were left without any Jewish experience. I wanted to offer a meaningful Jewish education for those children who for the mentioned factors did not receive it.

I worked in the schools of the congregations where Joel was the rabbi. I heard parents talk generally in sarcastic terms that Hebrew school was a wasted time. Some parents laughingly told their children of their own experiences that they learned close to nothing in their Hebrew schools and that they were frequently sent to the principal's office and they spent more time there than in the classrooms.

I did not believe that if I opened my own school, I would be in competition with the community's goals. I was firm in my decision. I wanted to provide quality education in fewer hours than the community school. My school quickly reached the maximum number of students I could handle. Parents also in surrounding communities welcomed the opening of my school. They came from tens of miles away from towns where only a few Jewish families lived. Local families enrolled their children, finding themselves in agreement with my concepts of Jewish education. My success was eminent. One of the principals of the community school made it his effort and goal in his own words, "I will eliminate the Ann Klein phenomenon." He was gone in two years. I spent many years in a happy atmosphere.

We found a pleasant side effect in my enterprise. I began teaching when the children reached second grade. They stayed with me and when they reached the age of religious responsibility, since their parents were not affiliated with any of the congregations, the Temples were not open for them for Bar- or Bat Mitzvah observances. The solution lay with the presence of my husband.

We cleared our ideas with the local rabbis to make sure that our moves were not perceived as competition with synagogue membership, and did not infringe on the natural rights of the religious and lay leadership. Accepting the invitation of our students' parents, upon completion of the requirements that were set in the curriculum, my school was able to offer the celebration.

In my eyes my students' accomplishments are real and convincing victories, or maybe a step further, maybe…even miracles.

My experience as a teacher covers a span of forty years. The Hebrews on their way to the Promised Land considered "forty years" a "long time." It has not been for me.

My admiration for my students gives me refreshing delight daily. For their sake, and for my fulfilment, I continue working with them. They inspire me to refine my goals, to adjust the curriculum, and to seek ways that suit their needs. When I see them strive, when I consult with their parents, I see obstacles overcome and my belief in 'miracles' confirmed.

Life is a series of ongoing miracles.

Just think along with me about the story of the Bumble Bee. According to all relevant theories of aero-dynamics which are proven by laboratory tests and in wind tunnel experiments with all kinds of objects, the Bumble Bee is unable to fly. The size, weight, and shape of the insect's body—in relation to its total wing spread—makes flying impossible for the Bumble Bee.

But…the Bumble Bee, being ignorant of these profound scientific truths, goes ahead and flies anyway - and manages to make a little honey every day!

BIND THEM FOR A SIGN

Ever since the day after my Bar Mitzvah–with the exception of a few days in deportation–I followed the commandment contained in Deuteronomy 6:8 and 11:18, "bind it as a memento on your arm and as a frontlet between your eyes." The English translation is not accurate because of a difference between the Hebrew and English usage of the second person pronoun. Hebrew differentiates between the second person singular and plural, English uses the same word "you."

Following the Hebrew text, I could say that the first version commanded every Jewish *individual* to bind the phylacteries-the English translation of the word tephillin-on one arm and between the eyebrows. The second version, the plural "you," insists that it is a binding commitment not only for the individuals, it is to be observed by the Jewish community. The biblical text also led me to know that the phylacteries are part of our Egyptian heritage. There it was used to describe a crown of the ruler and the gods. Placing them on my arm and forehead reminds me that my ancestors were slaves in Egypt, but through their liberation we are obligated to elevate ourselves to the highest religious and moral standards of royals. I read it also as a constant reminder that my observance expresses my loyalty to "teach these commandments to our children speaking of them constantly while I am at home, when I am away, when I retire for the night, and when I get up for a new day."

As Jewish life and practice developed different standards were adopted. Orthodox Jews usually practice the daily use of the tephillin. Lubavitsch volunteers in the United States or in Israel at airports, open markets, or street corners stop every man and strongly suggest putting on the prayer straps. Conservative Jews generally know the movement's attitude toward the use of phylacteries. The Reform prayer books include the commandment. These different standards created a great deal of confusion. Throughout our lives and careers the two of us became familiar with the challenges that we, a conservative rabbi and a teacher face. The practice of using the phylacteries at private prayers and congregational services has become a battle since members for various reasons do not attach any meaning to the tephillin and their use. At times it was dangerous to implement policies. Around contract negotiation times rocking the boat and strongly adhering to a principle can become hazardous to the livelihood of the rabbi and the family. Sometimes as a rabbi and a teacher we got into contradiction with coworkers and officers whose election and hiring were not based on their commitment to religious observance. The general confrontation can grow out of the congregation's culture. It has been our experience that practices to become accepted and followed must be supported by others, individuals and, above all, communities. It became evident to us that no suggestion, no teaching, no requirement would last if it was not part of the culture of the families and through them of the community. When our students reached the age of religious responsibility and became Bar or Bat Mitzvah we attempted to comply with our Conservative standards and taught putting on tephillin for the morning prayers *as the fulfilment of a commandment*. Besides the congregational culture that did not emphasize this aspect of fulfilling a commandment, the very difficult time in the life of a thirteen-year-old worked against our attempts. Being educators we have been aware of the teenagers resentment when we requested the use of the tephillin.

We have been amazed to experience that for the celebration parents and grandparents shopped for the most fashionable prayer shawls, head covering kippot, and bags for these items. But when it came to the purchase of phylacteries, commanded by the words of Moses on behalf of God, the resistance was significant. It suggested to us that they did not see the usefulness of these objects.

Many Jews attend Bar/Bat Mitzvah celebrations on Saturdays or on holidays as invited guests. Phylacteries are not donned on those days. Subsequently it is easy to consider that they are just objects that would be hidden somewhere behind the socks in a drawer never to be used. We heard another reasoning against the purchase of the phylacteries. The Bar Mitzvah has become a very expensive event. Invitations are ordered–picked out of the latest catalogues–with reply cards and envelopes that require return postage. Thee caterer has to be paid, flowers and centerpieces are needed, there must be two orchestras to suit the taste of the adults and the youngsters, photographers and the videographer make sure that the memories of the event will be kept and the relatives and friends would have the sets of pictures. We were more than once told that it was unjust to require the purchase of tephillin.

We found Bar Mitzvah photo albums very educational. Pictures of Israeli Bar Mitzvah boys, most of the times show the celebrant with the tephillin on his arm and on his forehead. American photo albums display the pose of the boy or the girl with an elaborate tallit and kippah, but not one picture with the phylacteries.

One grandparent brought to our attention a Bar Mitzvah Thank You card which told us another story of the tephillin. The grandson thanked him, "Grandpa, thank you for the pair of tephillin you bought for me. This week, Dad and I went to a mourner's home for the morning service, and I put on my new tephillin. I hope I will have many occasions like this to use it." This thank you note filled our hearts with sadness. The tephillin is a sign that we have a covenant, it is a reminder of the commandments that make us part of Jewish life. It is sad that it might turn into a reminder of death, and will be used only at services in mourners' homes.

Ann in her school environment and I in my rabbinic capacity faced the issue of congregational culture. We both operated in the belief that we could transmit knowledge and instruction to our students to prepare them for a life time as Jews, longer than the "one big day". We listened, corrected, and refined every word and every sound the children uttered to teach them an appreciation for a correct way and avoid mistakes. Then came the "big day." The grandparents, uncles and aunts came as invited guests. They accepted the "honors" to be witnesses to the public reading of the scriptural lesson. Aware of the possibility that they were not fluent in the "talking parts", we mailed them practice copies. The Bar or Bat Mitzvah recited the necessary prayers and assigned portions to perfection, and the invited family members apparently did not even spend a few minutes to practice what they were to recite. They mumbled and fumbled. Then we realized that there was very little appreciation for our students' efforts. They were told that they "did a wonderful *job*." But the adults "*performance*" did not match theirs. We painfully accepted the reality of our lives that our young people got used to the idea that all their efforts were really just for the big day.

The congregation's culture also taught them that the traditional requirement for Jews to pray three times a day on a regular basis has fallen into oblivion and the term "public services" acquired a new meaning. The general usage frequently calls, what is supposed to be the regular public prayer service, the "Bar Mitzvah Service." It is not a service in whose parameters the Bar Mitzvah celebration takes place. Our congregations did not hold regular Saturday afternoon services. But parents requested Havdalah Services-a ritual that differentiates the Sabbath rest from the days for work-to accommodate the Bar or Bat Mitzvah celebration. We experienced that in some cases these Saturday afternoon services lost their intended meaning when they were held in the afternoon and not around evening time. They hardly marked the separation between the observance of the Sabbath and the beginning of the weekdays.

The coming of age in the Jewish religious sense means that the person reached the age to observe the commandments that Judaism prescribes. It is an occasion to publically profess the acceptance of this responsibility in the course of a prayer service. We worked to change what the American Jewish usage turned into something different. This usage suggests a magician's act that on that big day the teenager is Bar Mitzvahed or Bat

Mitzvahed. To us it sounds like lifting the magic wand and make somebody something that the person was not before. But it seems that the magic usually does not work. Among us, rabbis, it is a serious statement that the Bar Mitzvah day is the last time the celebrant is seen in the synagogue. The same story is told in a not so serious anecdote. A rabbi asked for suggestions how to get rid of mice that appeared in the synagogue building. A colleague replied that he solved the problem in his place. He bought some cheese, placed it on the platform in the front of the Temple. Invited all the mice to a service. In the course of the service he "bar-mitzvahed" all of them. The mice had a wonderful party there, munching on the cheese spread and never again showed up in the building.

In some congregations the Bar Mitzvah observance has been replaced by *Confirmation* when a young Jewish person confirms belonging to that community and the decision to continue remaining faithful to its beliefs and practices. But according to the common usage the celebrant does not *confirm* his or her acceptance of this responsibility, the person is being *confirmed*. The Jewish person does not need to be confirmed. According to Jewish law—with some denominational differences—the person's birth parents' religious affiliation determines and confirms his or her religious affiliation. At a mature age that person has a right to confirm, or change that belonging.

THE SCHULE AT THE POOL

I am interested in customs, rituals, and social events. I am curious to learn their history and how they are observed or performed in the present. Our tradition holds that study is on the same level as worship and, if need arises, the synagogue can be sold to create funds for erecting a school.

I set aside time every day for study. I enjoy transmitting what I learned in my studies. I like teaching, mostly adults, and prefer to teach in informal settings. To teach in the synagogue building, even with chairs in a circle, felt more formal than I liked. I did offer informal learning sessions in private homes. Some of these courses attracted members of our congregation, also members of the other congregation joined us on a regular basis. The meetings in private homes circumvented the restriction that only temple members could attend. Most of the times, I led the study, but there were many capable people who on occasion volunteered to prepare a study session. At times more people attended our study sessions than prayer services.

I believed that if we could agree to meet for study in private homes, we could do the same to pray.

The Passover holiday's development was an important support to my thinking. The first stage was the celebration of the beginning of a new year by shepherds. It was observed by offering and consuming the Paschal lamb with one's immediate family for one night in the home, the tribal tent. If the family was not large enough to consume the lamb at one sitting, they shared it with their immediate neighbors.

When the pastoral life gave way to the agricultural farming society, the festival became a week-long celebration of the first grain.

When the Hebrews settled in their own country and a central government was established, a pilgrimage to the center of the Temple cult, to the capital city Jerusalem, was added to the new year celebration feast. The appearance in the capital city was to demonstrate the citizens' allegiance to the rulers and leaders of the theocracy.

These developmental stages indicated to me that initially and originally the central place for celebrations was within the circle of the immediate family. Even while a congregational rabbi, I kept this conviction in the fore of my practice. I consulted with families and proposed to consider the family celebrations in the home. I found meaning in repeating this form of celebrations. Four thousand years ago while families were small, the celebrations took place in the family's home. When the numbers became greater there was no way to accommodate all members there. There was a need for a larger room or hall. The synagogue was sensitive to these needs and besides being an edifice to conduct communal prayers and to house the school it became the building where social events were held.

Life is not stagnant, changes happen constantly. At times the changes redefine customs. At times they enhance the custom's spirit, at other times lead to a deterioration of the original intent. Some of my experiences pointed at the latter. Our families grew larger than a nuclear group. For celebrations they needed larger spaces than the homes could house. The synagogue provided the larger place and the availability allowed to consider new aspects. I frequently heard a statement that indicated this aspect when families planning celebrations of their lives' milestones considered the guest lists. They occasionally remembered that a member of the family was invited to the employer's home for dinner. The celebration seemed a good opportunity to reciprocate the invitation. Others might have thought that the celebration would be a good opportunity for a long-time-no-see relative to come and spend time with the family. With these and other important thoughts the list grew and became longer, but–in my mind–it moved farther away from the purpose of the celebration. I began consulting with families that they shorten the list and celebrate with family members for whom it was a significant event.

I was biased toward holding services in private homes, occasionally around festival dinner tables, removed from the synagogue.

When Ann opened her modest school, more opportunities opened to follow up on this idea. Although both congregations agreed to hold the Bar- Bat Mitzvah celebration of their members' children if Ann tutored them, this privilege was not granted to non-Temple members. Some of her students came from unaffiliated families. Knowing of my thinking, they approached me to offer services either in their home or at other appropriate locations. New Hampshire has appropriate facilities. One of them is an indoor and outdoor chapel in the scenic Monadnock region, the Cathedral in the Pines. The environment naturally adds to the inspiration and meditative mood for those who attend the Jewish and non-Jewish worship services held there on a regular basis. The chapel has all the necessary ritual objects available to us, the Ark, the Torah scroll, the pointer, the reading table, even the ususal head covering for men and women. I feel comfortable in that environment. Many of our students celebrated their becoming a Bar- Bat Mitzvah there.

The idea of holding services outside the confinement of the synagogue is not alien to me. It was strengthened when I passed a church during one of our vacations. The door was locked, but there was a note attached to one of the panels. I was curious. I stopped our car and went to read the note, "God is on vacation. Will see you in September." I was aware that in America activities slowed down for the summer months, so the mention of September did not seem to me unusual. I felt my frustration in the summer months already in three congregations. It was hard to gather the number of people required for public worship by our practice. We struggled, but did not consider God to be on vacation. The first sentence on that note just did not correspond to my understanding of an eternal God. The story in the Bible states that God stopped working only for one day after the completion of creation. I took the issue seriously. Using some humor, I followed the idea of the minister. I put a note at the door of our Temple, "God is not on vacation. We meet for services in your homes."

First I had a hard job with this proposal. If fate forced me to become a salesman, probably I never would have completed an order. I just did not acquire the skill to sell. But I needed people to go along with my idea. I began my advertising campaign. To my satisfaction and surprise, our members were quite willing to agree. The advertisement read, "The Schule at the Pool."

We planned and held services at the pool side, at the backyard, under the sun, and in the shadow. If the weather did not cooperate on Friday nights, the services were held in the living room. If not the living room, the patio was available.

The idea, the skeleton, was covered with flesh, and blood began flowing in the veins. Our services were held at an hour that did not clash with dinner time, the host family was home, and other worshipers came. Undoubtedly there was a pleasurable Sabbath spirit in the house, most probably in the hearts, too. Upon completion of the service on these Friday nights the host family remained home, but if their home was far from our house, I had a long stroll. I enjoyed the walk and the spectacular sunset in the fresh evening breeze. Our son was home from school, frequently he attended these services and we walked together. One weekend he decided not to go with me to the service, but offered to walk about half way to meet me. He kept his ward and I saw him at a distance. When he reached me, instead of the usual hug, he stopped and inspected me from top to bottom. I had no idea what he was looking for. He looked into my eyes and raised a question, "Dad, why are you wearing a suit, a shirt, a necktie, and a hat on this beautiful evening?" Almost indignantly I spoke, "I do it because this is what my congregants expect of me." He did not seem to accept my clear and self-evident answer when he continued, "But Dad, how about you? What do you think?"

I found that there is a side effect, if not a lesson, in everything. Monday morning, I bought my first sports jacket.

AS THE FAMILY GROWS

Just because I am who and what I am, some family events turned out bittersweet experiences. Our son finished his high school education. Time came for visiting college campuses and going to freshman orientation and initial interviews. Ann decided not to be part of these trips. The protecting father, who I was, feared letting the first-born to go by himself. I toured with him one of the big schools and the campus. I even sat on his side while he was interviewed. Our son spoke eloquently of his reasons for wanting to attend that school. His marks were more than good enough to be accepted. So I was shocked and surprised when at the end of the interview the dean said, "I have an advice for you. Go to college in Hawaii." The dean had much more experience than I. It took quite a while for me to realize that the suggestion was not directed to our son but at me with the hidden message, "Your son is an adult, he can stand on his own feet and speak for himself. Let him take charge of his life."

In spite of my presence at the interview, he was accepted to the school of his choice. A few days before the start of the semester I drove him there. I dropped him off at the curb, hugged him, kissed him, and drove away as fast as I could. My heart was heavy, my thoughts were rushing through my head. I worried what the small city boy would do in the metropolis away from his parents. I did not look back. I just watched him in the back view mirror of the car. I saw him, and I believed that he was there lost in the big city with his fears.

*   *   *

That was the father's experience. I, the mother, was weaker and I found it more difficult to deal with my emotions. I just did not want to bear my pain directly, experiencing the separation. Up to that day, I took care of the whole family. With his going to school the nest became half empty. The rooms in the house were quieter. I frequently opened the door to his room imagining that he was coming there. In the afternoon, automatically as a spontaneous reflex, I looked at the clock waiting for the hands to be in the position when the two of them used to come home from school. But now only one came. To control my urges, we made an agreement about the number of telephone calls coming home and going to school. I looked forward to our trips when we delivered the kosher meat to his freezer, alleviating my fears that he would not have enough to eat. It was nice to see that he did not lose weight due to starving, but his muscles became stronger, he consistently pursued his athletic activities. We enjoyed these visits, the exciting times when we saw him and went out with him for dinner.

*   *   *

The years flew by and before the junior year ended, he called and invited us to the house he rented with three other boys. This visit was different than the many others before. After being with him for a short time, he became fidgety, and said that he expected another visitor. She arrived, and the two of them announced their plan to get married before the next semester. They asked me to accede to their wishes and officiate as the rabbi at their wedding. I was happy that they asked me to perform the wedding but my joy was mixed with fears, "so young to be married, how will they manage the demands of married life and continue their studies?"

*   *   *

As expected and ususal, the mother's tears, both of joy and sadness, broke forth, hugs and kisses followed. My motherly tears soon gave way to invigorating planning. We were the parents of the groom, our contribution was to be minimal, but since the future bride's parents lived much farther, we could see her more frequently. I shared the female concerns about the wedding gown; I participated in the menu planning; I provided the list of guests on our side. I assumed it was a task I had to perform.

           *   *   *

The father's concerns concentrated on different aspects. I whole-heartedly wanted to welcome the new member into our family, to seek opportunities to get acquainted with her family, and involve them in the planning of the wedding. I had many premarital interviews. The new couples shared with me intimate details of their lives.

Already at the time this wedding in our family was planned, in my experience it was the rare exception that I would have not heard the answer, "It is the same" when I inquired about the residential address of the bride and the groom. Having had these experiences, I became increasingly uncomfortable to offer the benediction that was part of our traditional wedding ceremony. To avoid the actual sexual reference in that benediction even Philip Birnbaum toned down its wording in the English translation in his Daily Prayer Book, We offer our thanks to God, "who hast sanctified us with thy commandments, and commanded us concerning illicit relations; thou hast forbidden us those who are merely betrothed, and permitted us those who are married to us through consecrated wedlock."

In the course of our interview these young people did not consult me whether I gave them permission to have sexual relations before their marriage through the authority which my office as a rabbi represented. I considered our daily realities and long before our son's marriage I took the liberty to modify the words of the benediction which our predecessors composed in the realities and conditions under which they lived. Since the fourteenth century it has been customary to have a rabbi perform the wedding as a ceremony. I intended to continue this custom. My new words in the Hebrew benediction expressed the thought that we rabbis by the virtue of our ordination "were given the authority to preside over engagements and weddings."

The bride's family lived according to orthodox standards and belonged to an orthodox congregation. The wedding was planned to be in their home, in their backyard under the open sky. They felt obligated to invite their rabbi to the wedding. The day arrived. The skies were azure blue, the sun was shining, everyone was smiling. I was sitting alone in a corner in the house. But this is another issue, I will tell about it at another place.

     *   *   *

I saw my husband, the father-rabbi how withdrawn he was. I did not understand his behavior. I was too involved with my emotions. I was angry that he appeared removed from what was going on. I was certain that he had his reasons for his behavior and I did not want to intrude. It happened in the past that after resolving whatever was on his mind, he let me know about it. I busied myself with my thoughts and enjoyed thinking of the old saying, "if your son gets married, you gain a daughter." I searched the faces. They looked happy, and I was happy. I looked at the shining face of our son. He looked nervous as if he was looking for something. I thought that he was thinking of the privilege I had, and he did not, that I could go to the adjacent room and see his bride. I did not do that. The present showed a swarming moving crowd, guests hurried in and out. Some went to see the bride. On the screen of my mind I saw a different picture. It was like someone led me in guided imagery to a place where I was completely happy and very relaxed. For the moment, I felt the fulfilment of all mothers' dreams. My first-born was getting ready to establish a new home with his bride, and for us their future would mean a new home to visit and be part of it.

     *   *   *

The minutes turned into hours, the hours seemed as long as days. I do not know it for sure, but fathers probably are living in a different emotional world than mothers. My awareness was not there. I was in a different place. It took me several months to learn what many years later a book presented very convincingly that men are from Mars, women from Venus. With professional assistance I figured out what was going on in my emotional world on our son's wedding day. Therapy revealed that unconsciously I was experiencing the reduction of my powers. Our son, becoming a husband, would have the same powers I had, he would be more than a son. He would become equal with me. He would have the same rights and privileges, I had.

The long morning hours ended and the wedding was to begin. The guests found their chairs, the hum of conversations quieted down. I experienced a stage fright like that at the time of my very first public appearance. It took over my whole being. The greeting words of the wedding celebration were offered and it was time to recite the benedictions which I composed. Suddenly some noise accompanied a loud statement, "It is not a wedding." The orthodox rabbi rose from his chair with vehemence and hurriedly left.

*　　　　　*　　　　　*

The wedding day came to an end and we returned home. It was time to pick up my daily routine. But it was everything but routine. Our daughter, three years junior to her brother, was preparing to go to college. I became even more keenly aware than at the time her brother left for college that the nest will be really empty. It was of no help that we talked frequently about this generally known syndrome. Joel's simile did not console me. He repeated over and over again that we have been good parents, we were doing our job. Our home was the children's nest, and at that point in our lives we were like the bird parents standing on the edges and watch how our little ones began to fly on their own. I still feared that we were not the good parents we wanted to be. I was very young when we got married. I had no idea about parenting. It haunted me that I was robbed of my childhood by the events of World War II. I lost my father. I saw my mother struggle to provide for our family and keep us together. I jokingly but seriously said that we were growing up with our children. In the process, we consciously planned for the time when we would be again as we were in the beginning, just the two of us. We believed it was in our daughter's interest and for our sake to have a taste how it would be when she was going first to school and later–hopefully–when she would get married. We encouraged her to go on week-end retreats, be active in the conservative movement's youth organization. "Oh, mother." The conscious preparation proved to be incomplete, not very effective training. I missed the children already even if one was still practically on my side. I cried secret and not so secret tears. I was thinking and talking with Joel about the emptiness I felt and my desire to adopt a baby. The wish became stronger, but there was not much time to think. Time arrived for another preparation.

*   *   *

The time came, and I, the father, with certain ideas about conventions, was not prepared. One day the telephone rang. Ann picked up the phone and called me to do the same. Our daughter was at the other end. After a few words of light conversation, she "dropped the bomb." I knew that she was serious about a young man whom she met in the dorm when he visited her room mate. But I was not prepared for the words, "Mom and Dad, we decided to get married."

Mom was elated, jumped of joy. Congratulated our daughter, and with great curiosity wanted to know all the details, when, how, what was there for her to do, etc. I held the phone to my ear, but it seemed I forgot how to speak. Not a word came from me. The conversation went on just between the two of them. Three weeks passed, and I still did not say a word about the telephone call. Ann questioned my silence which she did not understand. I looked at her, and my facial expression said that I did not understand why she was not on my side. I, the father, thought from the early years of our daughter's life that she would come home with her fiancé to ask me, if not the two of us, for her hand. It did not happen. The world turned upside down. It was not enough that they did not come, the announcement came only as a telephone call, and she conveyed the news alone.

It took three weeks that I first heard the question, "What is it? Are you not excited, our daughter is getting married?"

I understood no matter how many years passed over my head, there was still much to learn. I woke up and worked hard to accept that the world is constantly changing. It was time for me to change with the times.

RESOLUTION OF A DILEMMA

In the usual sense, we were not an ordinary family. I had to take into consideration that our daughter's wedding was more than a family event. It was also a congregational event. We needed to consider this upcoming event in our lives seriously. Our son's first marriage, and the second after his divorce, provided no precedence to guide us in the solution of the problems we faced at this new turn of events. For those two weddings the bride's parents made most of the arrangements. Now we were the bride's parents, and most of the arrangements fell on my shoulders.

I talked to my mother and other mothers, I listened to their words, it still was difficult to arrive at a consensus. It was not just to decide about the menu and the wedding party. It was easy to do with our daughter's serious input. But there was the congregation, and we faced the question how to make up the guest list. We respected every member, but naturally not every member of the congregation was equally close to us. Some we wanted to be also at the wedding reception, not only at the Temple service. We could not have just them. If we invited them, I believed, rightfully all could have expected to be invited. That would have created an unsurmountable difficulty not only because of the expenses involved, but also because of the size of the auditorium, fire department regulation, and kashrut regulations. We have seen wedding receptions in other facilities. There the caterers were obligated to follow the practices of their ritual supervisors. It meant that the supervisor arrived at the hall with a torch and went through the entire kitchen to make it ritually acceptable, kosher. Not every facility agreed to that. Above all these issues, was my own issue. I was concerned that the receipt of the wedding invitation could be interpreted that we expected wedding gifts. I wanted to avoid this innuendo.

Initially all this preparation seemed overwhelming. But it was satisfying for me to see that we were able to divide the tasks. I was dealing with these issues, and Joel became involved with his tasks.

He resorted to one of his hobbies. He loved drawing and painting since his youth. He seemed rejuvenated when he decided to create a special ketubah, the Jewish wedding contract. He worked at the wedding service to make it special. Just as he concentrated to give a theme to his weekly Sabbath services, he coordinated the drawing of the marriage contract and the theme of the service. When I saw the completed Hebrew names of the bride and the groom drawn as the crowns of the king and the queen (our daughter's Hebrew name is the equivalent of the English "queen"), I wanted the reception to be a royal feast. To me it meant to celebrate it in the circle of our extended family and very close friends and at same time involve the entire congregation. It was a difficult task and I felt like applying the Hippocratic oath which medical doctors take, "do not do harm," in this case to our standing in the community. I divided the wedding into three segments. I planned the first segment to be the wedding ceremony. The sanctuary was large enough to provide seats to all who attended.

I took everything in a stride, a task to plan. It became much more when it was executed. When I entered the sanctuary as the mother of the bride, I relived the many occasions when I sat there alone silently meditating and dreaming before going to my classes. It was the realization of a great dream. I saw my young "queen" who was to establish her own little dominion. I saw myself as the future queen mother holding little babies, my grandchildren to my delight. I remembered Joel's disappointment that the "king" did not ask for the "queen's" hand in a personal appearance. He was there now with his parents. I saw them in my mental picture, probably having the same dreams I had. I heard the music that accompanied the measured steps of the attendants approaching the wedding canopy. It was adorned with flowers and lights as the young couple wanted it. I have seen my husband celebrating wedding services many times, but this time he appeared different. He seemed more nervous, more concerned. He was nervous at our son's wedding but somehow in a different way. There was a glow on his face. The first time the wedding day presented a struggle for him. Probably by this time he accepted the role of the parent to bring up the child and, when it was time, let the child go. In front of the Ark under the wedding canopy I saw three candles on the small table between him and the children. The bridegroom lit one candle at the beginning of the wedding ritual, then the bride lit the other candle. The bride and the groom lit the third candle in the middle candelabra with the joint flame of the two in their hands. While lighting the candle, their words expressed their intent to unite their two families into one with their warmth and love.

I began praying that these words become the realities of their lives together. I prayed under my tears also for those members of our families who were robbed by men's inhumanity to men and were not given life to see our happiness at this special service.

Then the dream came to an end. They kissed, I am sure not for the first time; they did not wait for the formal permission, "you now may kiss the bride," pronounced by her father as the clergy. It was not his style, he did not offer these words. The kiss came as a natural conclusion of an intimate special moment.

It was the time to see how the solution at which I arrived was at work. Every member of the congregation had been invited to the second part of the wedding, the reception and dance outdoors on the patio adjacent to the Temple. It was large enough to accommodate the swarming crowd. The wedding was in the afternoon hours giving ample time to mingle and for every member of the congregation to get acquainted with the members of both families who were just united through the marriage of their children.

As the hours passed, the movements became slower, the decibels of the cheerful noise lower, and the ones who were invited to the dinner found their way to the Temple's social hall. The kitchen did not have to be torched, it was recognized as kosher. Dinner time arrived, the best man raised his glass and made his toast. It was nothing special, but what followed it was. Not every daughter has the privilege and pleasure to walk to her father and say to the one who presided over her wedding service, "Thank you, Dad."

I did not know at that time how deeply significant this day was in our lives until several years later.

When we went through the hard times, the doomed and failed merger period, and just could not go back to that sanctuary, our daughter and family, as it was usual year after year, planned to join us for the high holidays. We were talking about our inner conflicts, our feelings and reluctance, she turned to us. "Mom and Dad, I understand your hurt, but for me it is all different. At age thirteen I celebrated my Bat Mitzvah at that Temple. When I was in high school, I led junior services at that chapel. I had my wedding in front of the Ark in that synagogue. When our first child was born, after his circumcision in your home, we attended the Saturday morning services to celebrate his naming in Israel's religious and ethnic community. That Temple is my Temple."

It's Ten O'clock. Do You Know Where Your Children Are?

For the two of us, who are survivors of the European Holocaust, having children, has been a special gift. To live to see the birth of grandchildren is a special privilege.

I lost my father even before he would have had a chance to take me down the aisle at my wedding. One of the few memories I have of him is his frequent expression and fervent prayer to live the time of becoming a grandparent. We were five children in the family, his wish really did not have any special meaning to me. But when the time came to see my grandchildren, my mother's teaching came to life, "The children are the investment and the grandchildren the dividends."

The first time I held our first grandchild in my arms, I felt like I was communicating with angels. Without any nostalgia I can say that he became my protecting angel. He was only six months old when I was hospitalized with an unknown ailment. There was no diagnosis. We faced the threat that the physicians might not devise a treatment plan that would cure my illness. Then one day our daughter appeared in the door of hospital room with the little blue bundle in her arms. She walked in, put a blanket on the floor, and I saw my angel crawling. Whatever my health condition was, I decided that I had to make it. It was difficult. But he continued watching over me. I was not aware that our daughter left an enlarged photo of this little boy in our home with Joel. Our daughter had to go back to her job after the short three-day visit. The next day Joel brought in the large framed picture and placed it on the window sill. I could see him any moment. He smiled back at me every time I looked into his eye on that picture. Once I said that my mother gave me life

163

twice, our first grandson brought me back from the arms of a devastating illness. I gained my life for the third time.

I recovered and was blessed with the generosity of his mother and father. Whenever we wanted to have him for a week or a weekend with us, we could simply pick up the child and take him to our house. The same pleasure was extended to us later when his brother arrived.

I am a selfish grandmother. I love our grandsons, but I constantly dreamed of something pink. At every visit in a mall or a store, I was drawn by the baby clothes and looked at outfits for little girls. When I learned that our daughter expected for the second time, for months I was convinced that our next grandchild would be a girl. Just about the time when we expected the great moment, early morning the phone rang, and our son-in-law whispered, "we have a boy." I could not contain myself and very loudly asked, "What?" When I realized what feelings I might have evoked, quickly I regained my composure and was able to congratulate him on the joyous event.

I marvel at the relationship we grandparents have built with our grandchildren. It has been an additional benefit that saw how it changed my relationship with our children. I had doubts about my ability to parent our children. I was not alone with this frightening feeling. One time, our daughter called when I was at home alone and said that she needed to talk with me. In tears she questioned me whether it was possible to love a second child as much as the first. She did not know how she could divide her love to be enough for her two sons. I learned a suitable answer from my self-doubting and from reading. I read somewhere that mothers do not divide their love for their children, they multiply it. Our daughter appreciated hearing that this simple wisdom lifted my spirit when I worried about my ability to love her as much as I loved her older brother. Her tears turned into smiles whenever she recalled our conversation.

Our son had no children from his first marriage. Eight months after the birth of our daughter's second son we welcomed their first-born of his second marriage. Two brothers followed him. As happy as I was with our growing family, it was not easy to bear that the three of them lived much farther than the two here in the States. They live beyond the borders. The trip is much longer than the two-hour drive to our neighboring state. But they manage their visits. They cannot be frequent. They make them longer.

As we considered it a God-given privilege to see our grandchildren, it was even a greater privilege to enjoy the times when my mother was with us at the time of their visits. I did not dare to believe that I would be blessed to see four generations together after the devastation of my family by the European Holocaust. The love and caring of the children and grandchildren for my mother left an indelible mark in my memory. She frequently suffered from arthritic pain. The doctors suggested to apply heated towels at the painful areas of her leg. Our third grandson watched this procedure. When Omama had some pain, usually she lay down on the sofa. One afternoon my mother rested lying on the sofa, and the little one, about two-and-a-half, drew close to her and looked at her leg. He saw that she had only stockings on her leg. Suggesting that it was time for the treatment, he immediately yelled after me in the other room, "Omama, towel."–I believe he will grow up to become a doctor.

*　　　　　*　　　　　*

In retrospection it is clear to me that having grandchildren changed my life, I became a better parent.

While preparing for my advanced therapy training, I entered psychotherapy. To have a larger picture of me and how I related to others, the psychiatrist invited Ann to our sessions. In one of our conjoint sessions, our therapist inquired about our son. We talked about our close relationship, about the frequency of our visits with him in college, the frequency of letter exchanges and telephone calls. When the therapist said that it would be helpful if we allowed him to establish his full independence, his words reminded me of the dean's comment that he should go to college as far from our home as Hawaii. Therapy pointed out that he meant more to us than simply being our son. Our unconscious unjustified protectiveness represented that he was a replacement for those whom we lost during the Holocaust. It was a hard lesson. It was even harder to accept and integrate it that we could trust his abilities, and give him the space to grow.

My anxious thoughts frequently reoccurred that our children would not have enough experience, and I would not be available to help them.

When our first grandson was born, my fear overshadowed my joy. From the moment we followed his parents on the way home from the hospital where he was born, I re-experienced my troubling thoughts. After we left their house for the two-hour drive home, I was much quieter than usual. The two hours seemed much longer on the road than they really were. I worried about who would take care of him when he would be sick, like any child at times. Would his parents have the necessary information to take care of his needs? The first calm moment came upon me when I answered my own questions. It was my realization that we were very young parents, had no training in parenting, and no grandparents in the immediate vicinity to call upon when illness or other problems arose. Our children grew up, we took good care of them. I told myself that I must trust our children's abilities to care for their children the same way we did. Becoming a grandfather, I became a much better parent. I reminded myself that becoming a good parent meant that I did not have to know where our children were at ten o'clock at night. I learned to trust them and allow them to follow their instincts and their plans for their lives. When I became a grandfather, I came to see how helpful it was to me when at one time our son came home from college with a large notebook under his arm and told us that he wanted to talk with us. When we settled, he opened his book and presented a plan for his future. We listened attentively and when he finished what he had to say, I took the floor first. Remembering the details he presented, I made my remarks and wanted to enlighten him, "If you do this, that would happen, if you do this, this will not happen; if you don't do that this will happen, if you don't do that, this would not happen." We continued, and he listened to his mother's words just as carefully as he followed my words. Then came his question, "Dad, how do you know all this?" Feeling that my authority was threatened, almost indignantly I replied, "From experience." He calmly and modestly turned to us, "Mom and Dad, this is the only thing I want from you, let *me* have the experience."

When I heard his words, apparently I forgot how only three years before that event, I solved another problem. I learned that American parents usually offer a long talk to the child who is about to leave for college. When I went to college, I continued to live at home. My father did not have to prepare me for the time when I would have begun using my independence. I had no model to follow. The time came threateningly close, and I did not have much to tell our son before he left for school. I had no big speech to deliver. It was unlike my professional life. For the preparation of sermons and lectures I used ample time. I did not use the years of our son's life to prepare for his first departure from home. When the three of us sat together, in desperation I turned to him and said. "You have lived with us for almost eighteen years. We, your parents, provided you with a model for a life style. You have three choices: you can accept and follow it; you can drop it and create your own; if it does not fit, you can alter it to your liking." I intended to communicate that we trusted him. But it seems, that during the few years that passed since I said those words, I lost my full ability to trust our children's judgments. The arrival of grandchildren each time served as remedial courses in trusting. I learned my lesson well. They established their professional and private lives on the foundation of their believes and practices. Maybe there is another lesson in this: Children grow up despite their parents.

THEY WILL COME TO YOUR HOLY MOUNTAIN

Both of us were ardent Zionists from our early childhood years.

After returning from the concentration camps, as a young girl, I joined the Shomer organization's youth program although it was not favorably looked upon by my family members who adhered to the orthodox standards. But one of the group leaders happened to be my mother's cousin. Although this cousin came from a generally secularist family, my mother knew him and trusted him. Her concerns were mitigated by her belief that he would not turn me against her beliefs no matter what direction the movement represented.

*   *   *

My involvement with the Zionist movement began when I was eight years old. I joined the organization that was active in my childhood community. I marched in the city's park with my peers in the Betar movement to practice our "military preparedness." By the time I reached high school age, my knowledge of Zionism broadened and I chose the youth cell of a centrist Zionist organization. I enjoyed the lessons about Jewish and Zionist history and had a taste of learning Hebrew as a living language. The upper classes of high school I attended at the Seminary. This schooling moved me toward the religious segment of Zionists, the Mizrachi that set its goal to establish Israel as a spiritual and cultural center for world Jewry.

My ideal, my mentor, my rabbi did not favor our Zionist orientation. He was an ardent anti-Zionist on ideological basis. First he appreciated the emancipation of the Jews in our country and firmly believed that we had to be loyal citizens of the country which recognized Judaism as a religion and emancipated us as citizens. He expressed his opposition to Zionism as a historian in private conversations and preached to his congregation that Jews and Judaism survived the millennia because we lived in a diaspora. He believed that there was a danger in the ingathering of Jews into one country because the concentration might have made it easy to annihilate our people. He did not accept the idea of peoplehood of Jews either, but he used the term, Jewish people, anyway. History meted out a change of heart for him. I know from witnesses that close to the end of his death in the concentration camp, he said that if he ever survived he would be a Zionist and a supporter of the idea of establishing a State for the Jewish people. He did not live to see the year 1948.

My rabbi's opposition did not influence my dreams and plans. I always contemplated the possibility of moving to Israel. But I am human. While I was a student, my father's ideas directed many of my steps I took and the decisions I made. He instilled in me that before embarking on a new task, I had to complete the one in which I was engaged. So–I believed–I had to complete my education before I could think of that move. When I reached that goal, my filial obligation stopped me. My father's physical condition, the result of a deficiency in his bone structure that he acquired in the concentration camp, held me back.

*　　　*　　　*

When I got married, Joel and I shared the goal of a possible move to Israel. But the Russian occupation resulted in lowering the Iron Curtain and sealing off the borders. The plan and the goal thinned to a vague hope. We longed to get out of the prison which our country became, and I vowed that if ever a chance would arise, after crossing the borders, the only place I would move would be Israel. We maintained constant contact with the Israeli authorities through their consulate even if the risk was great. We received our collective visa and our name was included in the list of prospective emigrants.

The long awaited opportunity presented itself. Five rabbinic students, some married some single, and we received permission from the Hungarian government to leave the country within a strictly defined short period of time. But we had a very serious problem. I was pregnant. We thought that with some manipulation we could extend the validation of our exit visa. While hoping that it might happen, our son was born, and I had serious health problems for six weeks immediately after childbirth. Besides that, when I was not able to produce mother milk and our son needed it according to medical advice, we had to buy it from other nursing mothers. The long journey to Israel was filled with great unforeseen difficulties. We were not assured that our needs could be met on the route and later after our arrival to a country where newcomers lived in temporary huts and tents. We learned from letters of new arrivals that when opportunities arose they had to move to places where they were directed. The country needed mostly agricultural workers. I did not dare to subject our child and myself to the unknown conditions and instability.

We stayed, and the extension of the permit to leave was denied. When the Hungarian uprising against Russian communism opened the borders, I made a decision to leave with the children even if it meant to leave Joel behind whose fate at that time was unknown.

*   *   *

When finally I escaped and learned that my family already reached the United States, I did not want to abandon my dream and commitment to my Zionist ideology. I began my letter writing campaign. One letter after the other from Austria emphasized to Ann our promise that if ever the borders opened there would be only one destination for us, Israel. When Ann's replies came, I was puzzled. She forthrightly refused even to hear about her return to Europe and join me to realize our idealized plans. She mentioned that she just left one war with the children, and was unwilling to enter another battlefield. Due to the news black-out in Hungary, I had no idea that she was writing about the 1956 Sinai campaign. She was determined to stay, and her determination brought me, too, to the United States. This country gave us opportunities which–we believe–no other country could have. But since we became free people, the road remained open, and if not to settle in Israel, it became possible to visit and spend expanded periods of time there.

*   *   *

It was a firm decision on our part that the sweet-sixteen birthday gift to our children would be an El Al round trip ticket. Our son enjoyed the peaceful era of the summer of 1966 when Israel was still in her early years and enjoyed the admiration of the international community which looked upon the small David who defeated Goliath in an almost miraculous way. Our daughter spent her summer of 1969 still in the mood of euphoria within the borders of the country which later earned the designation by some as the Greater Israel. We had the good fortune to spend our summer of 1968 with some distant Israeli relatives and very close friends. Not all the people whom I now call friends were familiar and known to me, I inherited them from Joel who built a close relationship with them. But as it happened, they mean so much to me that I have a hard time to put it into words value of these relationships.

*   *   *

The first six months of my American life we lived in New York. I was engrossed in my English studies when I realized that having been captured near the border between Hungary and Austria and my subsequent imprisonment left me with a painful experience. I prided myself for my excellent memory and all of a sudden I could not recall names, dates, personal relations and had great difficulty to connect the material of my new studies to information which was available to me before. I suffered partial amnesia. I was frightened by this realization. By having damaged capability to remember I needed more energy to learn new material and to translate previously known material into my new second language. One of my three childhood friends who left Hungary before the Iron Curtain fell unknowingly helped me in my terrifying condition in Haifa. When this friend left Hungary illegally, his mother stayed behind. Through manipulation and under the right of family reunification, she obtained a legal passport and visa. She took her son's pride possession, his pictures with her. For our first stay in Israel in 1968 we rented an apartment on the street where they lived and spent almost a month with them. He showed me his photo albums. The pictures contained a great portion of my past. He told me the stories that were connected with the pictures of my childhood, friends with whom we spent most of our free time. These images saved anew on my mental hard drive slowly brought back some of the lost memories. My friend made copies of my family members' pictures, my mother, my father, my brother which I took with me when we returned home.

This friend proved to be a life saver without any ceremony and pretense. That one month in Israel strengthened our friendship. It became much stronger than ever before. We remained true life-time friends.

In previous chapters we wrote about my other friend, my very close relationship with him, and the admiration I had for him. He, too, lived in Haifa with his family at the time of our first visit in Israel. He came to Lod Airport with my other friend to greet us there. On our way to Haifa, he gave us clear instructions what we could discuss when we will be in his home. He informed us that his wife cannot stand that we, or, for that matter, anyone had the guts to work and made a life easier than theirs. He spoke of his children, their education and angrily said that in Israel there were no scholarships available for young people, it was not easy to go to school, etc. He said that when his wife would hear us talking about these subjects, she would be "honest to the extent that it would hurt." On the fourth day of our visit to Israel, we experienced the truth of his instructions.

We erroneously assumed that the details of our families' lives would be of great interest to them since our son spent the month after his sixteenth birthday with them, and the following year their daughter stayed with us in the USA.

In Israel I kept a detailed diary. I made an entry in my journal every day. About our first visit with them I found the following statement, "In our conversation all issues were avoided. We were not allowed to speak of our son's scholarship, his achievements in school. Whatever we said, was met with angry answers that revealed their jealousy."

My friend provided me with another surprise. When we grew up, I saw that their home was not particularly observant. I spent some time with him on the beach in Haifa the day before we visited them in their home. I learned that he became strictly observant, and belonged to one of the Hasidic groups. For about an hour we talked about Israeli and American politics and religious issues. Having lunch with him and seeing that I recited the short form of the thanksgiving after the meal, he told me that he would not tolerate my short form of the grace in his home. But I saw the rote repetitive manner he recited his long form, it took much less time to finish it than my short prayer. It surprised me that he was even joking and interrupted his prayer by funny remarks. Since he repeatedly interrupted, it was difficult to discuss our position on religious issues, it still became clear that he looked down on the Conservative and Reform approaches to Judaism. But although his practice expressly was orthodox, his thinking was in line with the reform ideology. His official standing and his job opportunity as an art teacher in a religious school would not allow him to see and say it.

It was similarly disappointed by religious practices at other places, too. We spent a Shabbat in the home of another friend from my youth. He was ordained also by the Seminary, our Alma Mater. We went to the services in his neighborhood synagogue. I felt depressed because in the service nothing revealed the reality of Israel. As far as the service was conducted I could have been in Kiev or Williamsburg. It was not any different. My idea of prayer service was contrary to that experience. The prayers of the leader followed a rote repetition The prayers were the same that were recited since the time a prayer book was created. The noise was loud. Conversations about business and family events interspersed the pre-scribed prayers. Hardly anybody paid attention to follow the prayer leader. There was no dignity, no regard to communal prayer. Although my friend was ordained a neolog (closest to the far right of the American conserva-tive) rabbi, he attended services at that place that followed the Sepharadi, oriental orthodox rite.

I wrote in my diary about another synagogue service in Beer Sheva, "We went to the People's Beth Ha-Midrash on Friday night. The Rabbi was the son of a rabbi. He studied Talmud with his father, and that qualified him for the position. He and some of his congregants wore their shtraimle and kapotke. Practically all people, nineteen adults and eight youngsters, were Hungarian. I found it interesting that in Hungary they spoke Yiddish, their "momme loshen (mother tongue)" because Hungarian was not holy enough; in that synagogue suddenly they all spoke Hungarian. What both-ered me was that the twenty-seven people behaved the same way in their synagogue in Beer Sheva as they did in their small towns in Hungary. Similarly to the service in Haifa, there was no recognition of the fact that they lived in Israel and were supposed to speak the language of the Land, Hebrew. There was no concern for the visitor who might have wanted to fulfil his need to pray. I became so frustrated that I felt sick to my stomach."

While in Beer Sheva we paid a visit to the large oriental family into which Ann's brother married. One member of that family was the rabbi-schochet-mohel (slaughterer of animals for kosher consumption-performer of circum-cision), and operated a grocery store in the community. Around the dinner table his daughters talked about the different categories of observant Jews in Israel. They expressed very little interest in religious life or ritual observances despite their father's position. The nephew of the rabbi listened to our con-versation with his uncle about his views on religion and his relation with the religious authorities. Later he confided in me that he did not like the rabbi because he did not live up to his words.

From Beer Sheva we took the bus to Jerusalem. On the way we talked very little until the arid, dusty, dry landscape of Beer Sheva and the desert was behind us and approaching the city we caught the beautiful scenery, the breath-taking panorama. The heavy traffic moved slowly on the four- and six lane highway. Our eyes were kept on the burnt-out armored trucks and tanks left on the roadside as lasting memorials of 1948 attack on the newly established State. I was full of expectations, I could hardly wait to catch the first sight of the city. At the bus terminal my high school class-mate, my other close friend met us. Seeing him brought back the memory of summers when either I spent a month with his family or he came to stay with us. While we lived in the mid-west serving a congregation in the Chicago area, we had an opportunity to renew our friendship while he pursued his studies toward his Ph.D. at the University. He was more than my classmate at that time. He was the deputy minister of education in charge of the public schools' curriculum development. He drove us through the new city and along the walls of the old. The view was breath taking. It was marred only by the sight of the desecrated cemetery on Mount Olives which has been already in reconstruction. We took the Via Dolorosa, visited the Arab market, entered the Omar Mosque and walked down to the Kotel Ma-aravi, the Western Wall below the Temple Mount. As we approached the wall, I took some pictures. I was a tourist. I did not seem or feel touched by the sacredness of the place. I remained cold. I could not understand that I was not caught by the excitement which lived in me for years preparing myself for that moment. I read ancient and medieval travelers accounts of their moments when they first caught sight of the only remaining part of our Jerusalem Temple. I prayed daily for the ingathering of our people, the rebuilding of the Holy City. I was not cap-tured by the sight. I stepped into the prayer area; recited three psalms appropriate to the occasion that I have reached the holiest place of my people. I was still cold. I moved a few steps closer. I stopped as if my foot could not carry me farther. There I was. I stood close to the wall after being three times close to death: once in the concentration camp, a second time when I received a death sentence from a hostile nation's military court, and my third close brush with death was when I had a blood infection following surgery. I was awed by the thought that I had been granted this privilege. I recited the Kaddish by myself in memory of my martyred mother. In a flash I visualized her who in her entire life longed to come and see this wailing wall. In my imagination I saw six million others of whom many had the same longing, but were not allowed to live the day and have the same chance that I had.

I took a few more steps closer to the wall. I became weak. I lost control. I touched the edge of a stone block. I was leaning against the wall, my tears broke forth and I cried silently for no apparent reason. I could not describe my feelings and could not find a reason for my feelings. I turned around and left the place. Ann already waited for me beyond the iron fence that separated us, men and women. She asked how it was for me finally reaching this destination. I could not answer her, the lump was still blocking my throat. Our friend also came back to meet us. After a long silence, finally, I could talk about neutral subjects and asked questions about where his car was parked and how far we had to walk. I asked only for one thing, not to visit any other site on that day. If we did, it would have been a tremendous let-down for me.

I wanted to avoid the let down. I succeeded on that day, but not the following night. During this visit, as my diary reveals, I was preoccupied with religious issues and wanted to hear what Israelis think and see how they live out their religiosity. During our stay in Jerusalem, we had the opportunity to reunite with five other graduates of our Seminary. None of them filled rabbinic positions in Israel. They were university professors, high school principals, and administrators. Our conversation was not at all different than any others many years before. They turned to us and asked about the different Jewish movements in America. I had no chance to answer their inquiries since they seemed to answer their own questions.

I listened and accepted their conviction that they were more familiar with Jewish life in North America than we. So I allowed them to take over, and stopped talking. On the way from this gathering Ann and I talked that we both felt like time stopped. The evening reminded us of our wedding reception, vacations in the villa on the lake with rabbis, and our reunions in Haifa. My colleagues seemed convinced that they knew everything better, no one was as perfect as they, and they had nothing to learn anymore.

*   *   *

Joel had no close relatives in Israel. For me our first visit to Israel was a momentous event. My brothers left our home for Israel twenty years before. I had not seen them and very rarely corresponded with them throughout those years. I was very excited anticipating the reunion with the older one who settled in Israel.

Although we rented a car, I did not allow Joel to drive on the Israeli roads after I had heard of the many accidents and tragedies. He reluctantly agreed and returned the car. The public transportation was good, and friends offered rides to take us wherever we wanted to go. The shadow of the pulpit followed me to Israel, too. First we visited Joel's friends and his only living relative, his second cousin. He was a general in the Israeli Defense Forces, fought in three wars, was wounded three times, and at the time of our visit was the chief of security in the southern region. We spent a day and a night in his home. I mentioned to him that the next day we planned to visit my older brother in Beer Sheva. He spontaneously offered to take us in his jeep. The trip was relatively short, and I was preoccupied with my expectation to be with my long-time-no-see brother and his family. The general did not need directions, he knew exactly where to go and where to stop. He jumped out of his jeep. I followed him on my wobbling legs with my heart in my throat. He rang the bell, and when the gate opened a loud voice brought me back to reality. I saw my brother and Joel's cousin fall on each other's shoulder hugging. I could not believe my eyes. I was standing there, waiting to see my brother, and he was hugging a man, the driver who took us to his house. I saw their tears and heard them saying how wonderful it was to see each other again. After we had our hugs and kisses, I found out from their stories that while waiting in Italy for a ship to take them to Palestine they met and established a friendship. Israel surely is a small country, but after this incident no one could ever tell me that the whole world is not small.

I had difficulty to relate to my brother. It was not that I felt ignored in the initial minutes. Twenty years of absence tied our tongues. Slowly we filled the gap. He talked about his adventures in the world after he left our home. To hear about the hardships and difficulties he faced made it more vivid for me to understand the hardship of those who attempted to reach Palestine before the State of Israel was established. It was unlike watching the movie, Exodus. His life was hard in the newly established Israel, too. He could not find employment in the trade he learned in Europe. By the time of our reunion he seemed to have steady employment. He was a chef at the local air force base. He worked hard on an almost unpredictable schedule. The pilots had to be fed before each take-off. While we were there a wide-spread military training exercise was conducted. When he had to work we could talk only late in the evening leading into the wee hours of the day. We talked about recent events, it still was inevitable that we turned to our childhood. He was a brilliant student. He studied the religious books, he saw our parents' way of life. I was interested and asked him about the change which we had seen already in his home, that there was no sign of religious observance.

He shed light on this issue when he answered my questions. He told me about the painful Saturday afternoons. He hated our father's weekly examinations of his studies. He feared the punishment that followed an incorrect reply. Being on his own in his wanderings, he had no chance to observe the religious laws. His faith broke, he altered his beliefs, and got further away from religious observances.

I asked him about the time when his then-very-young son would reach school age. "What would he learn about Judaism, Jewish religion? What kind of awareness would his son gain of the heritage that was his and mine?" He had no hesitation. The man, who was brought up in our orthodox home, told me that it mattered to him and would matter to his son that they lived in Israel, that they lived in that country and defended it even if the price would be the sacrifice of their lives. That was his religion and Judaism. In his belief they did not need the religious laws which were set down hundreds and thousands of years before his life. The reality of Israel's life was his reality, and Israel's realities dictated the directions he followed.

My brother married the daughter of a Moroccan rabbi who became the widowed wife of an oriental man. From her practices I learned a great deal about a Judaism that was different from mine. I met her extended family and her two sons of her previous marriage. The warmth, their hospitality, and the family's cohesion gained my sincerest admiration. I felt the warmth of their close-knit family, and unexpectedly I felt becoming part of a larger family.

We were not aware that my older sister was visiting Italy with her daughter at the time of our visit to Israel. In the small town, where the small grocery store was the post office and the telephone company, it was a sensation that we received a telegram from my sister. It was only for the goodness and friendship of the grocer that we got it just before my sister and niece arrived for a short stay. I was happy that we, the three siblings, and some of our children could be together and feel part of a large extended family.

Our trip reunited us not only with family and friends. It connected us with the history of our people. Joel's interest took us to the excavation of an ancient synagogue at nearby Tel Arad. It was an unforgettable experience to walk on the soil where our ancestors saved the belief in one God from oblivion. It was unique to be in a country where the world's treasure, the Bible, could be literally our written tour guide. For me above all it was a chance to see some of my relatives who were saved from the ravages of the European and Israeli wars and lived a new life. I visited my second cousins with whom I shared painful and happy times in the years that were behind us. I could hug and kiss my aunts who were my hosts in the summers of my life's early years. We exchanged old stories and told each other new ones.

That visit reenforced my strength and support that is expressed in the words of a song, "Am Yisrael Hai", "Our People Is Alive" and made a blooming garden in the desert sand.

THE LAST, BUT NOT THE LEAST

We are acutely aware that it has been your choice to read this book, so we thank you for taking the time and allowing us to share with you some of our experiences and stories of our lives. We truly appreciate it. It is our hope that through these simple stories and anecdotes about parts of our professional and private life, you have discovered some truths about your lives as individuals and members of communities, whether you are in professional, communal, or religious institutional relationships.

We learned what Ray Bradbury once wrote, "If we listened to our intellect, we'd never have a love affair. We'd never have a friendship. We'd never go into business, because we'd be cynical. Well, that's nonsense. You've got to jump off cliffs all the time and build your wings on the way down."

We entered our marriage and our professions with our dreams and aspirations. After several decades they are all still important for us. They give meaning to our lives.

We took risks all along our lives's journey and when we decided to offer these vignettes to the public. We took risks and we did it in a loving, playful way, as passionately and humanly as we could.

Community life is like a family's life. It is all about relationship. It is an old adage that we do not learn from somebody else's experience. We all need to have the experience ourselves. Our life is not different than yours. You might have had the same or similar experiences. If that is the case you can relate to what we wanted to say and you might have learned from it. If you did, you already made important steps toward improving your own and your community's relationships.

It is the final chapter of this book. In closing we add the two most important words in every relationship, "thank you." To some people who touched our lives, we said our "thank-you". To some others we might have forgotten to verbalize what we felt in our soul and heart. This is the time to fill those gaps. You have read in these chapters about events that enriched our lives. Every incident was an enrichment since we were determined to make them a learning experience. We are grateful for every lesson. We offer the two words on these pages to those individuals, couples, and families who made a difference in our relationships.

We carry in us the gratitude for the president's wife who waited on the driveway of our new home to greet and welcome us into the community where we spent some of the happiest years.

The number is more overwhelming than either I or Joel could thank everyone who came to assist the family when he was in the hospital. These were the significant examples of life' curious ways that not the heroic and brave actions make the expression of caring. The small things, the milk, coffee, and muffins that were brought to our house that gave us time to concentrate on other tasks. The unselfish and surprise appearances to take our children to kosher homes to have a family dinner when we were not available; the quiet times provided when one of us was in the hospital, or when one of us was grief-stricken by the loss of a family member, created lasting memories even just by holding our hand.

We cannot forget the group of people who believed that injustice was done by a small but vocal minority and banded together to reverse a decision. We cannot forget the individuals who enriched our lives with their goodness.

Among our fondest memories we keep our gratitude to the physician who remained true to his oath when our daughter fell ill and had a high fever. We felt helpless in the middle of a relentless snow storm. Instead of the usual suggestions about "take two aspirin and call me in the morning", or "take her to the hospital's emergency room," he took his car, drove in the snow storm, and made a house call to ease the pain of the child and restore her parents' peace of mind.

We could not thank him at that time, but now we offer our thanks to our friend, the "rabbi of rabbis and the anonymous helper of widows and the isolated" who took upon himself to come to our community to conduct negotiations when our strength was not efficient to convince individuals and a committee to represent our right.

The pulpit cast a long shadow in our lives and in the life of those who stand or sit in the height of some authority. But there is no shadow, in which there would not be some light, especially a guiding light. We concentrated on the light.

In our philosophical moments we talked and searched for the nature of God. This English word and similar words in other languages, expresses our idea that God is Good. But God is also the totality of the Universe. The Universe is not perfect, therefore there must be room for some imperfection in the essence of God, too.

We both read a Hungarian novel about the biblical Noah. When after the flood subsided, he left the ark, and, as his first gesture, gave thanks and offered a sacrifice in gratitude for the lives saved in the ark.

The novelist raised the issue that there was no expression of sadness and mourning in Noah's acts for all those, the rest of the world, who perished.

A large part of our world vanished and caused cruelty, suffering, and sadness. The story of our lives includes this dark side. But inside us is the bright spark, the divine power that moves us toward constant improvement. That goal survived in us. On occasions we could see that goal in the distance. We give thanks for those vivid moments of peace.

If you related to some of our trying moments described in these short chapters, we reached part of that goal. We wanted to show that in the darkness of every trial and tribulation there is that shining point which taught us to find the way not only to survive, but live a full, and fully satisfying life. For all that is bright and dark, cloudy and clear, we give thanks since we found peace.

We search for ways to reach it every day.

ABOUT THE AUTHORS

Joel T. Klein, Ph.D., an ordained rabbi, is a licensed pastoral psychotherapist. He served congregations in Hungary and the USA for thirty years. He maintains a private practice for individual, couple, and family therapy.

Ann Klein's initial training was nursing in hospital setting. Her marriage to a rabbi led her to pursue additional studies, became a teacher and school principal. These experiences qualified her to open her private school for Judaic studies.

The couple has two children and five grandsons.